Sacred
Speech

Other SkyLight Paths Books by Rev. Donna Schaper

Labyrinths from the Outside In:
Walking to Spiritual Insight—
A Beginner's Guide
(with Carole Ann Camp)

Sacred Speech

A Practical Guide for Keeping Spirit in Your Speech

Rev. Donna Schaper

Walking Together, Finding the Way
SKYLIGHT PATHS Publishing
Woodstock, Vermont

Sacred Speech:
A Practical Guide for Keeping Spirit in Your Speech

Grateful acknowledgment is given for permission to use "God Weeps" by Shirley Erena Murray, copyright © 1996, used by permission of Hope Publishing Co.

Library of Congress Cataloging-in-Publication Data
Schaper, Donna.
Sacred speech : a practical guide for keeping spirit in your speech / Donna Schaper.
        p.   cm.
Includes bibliographical references.
ISBN 1-893361-74-8 (hardcover)
1. Conversation—Religious aspects.   I. Title.
BL629.5.C67S33   2003
291.5'672—dc21
2002154856

10   9   8   7   6   5   4   3   2   1
Manufactured in Canada

SkyLight Paths Publishing is creating a place where people of different spiritual traditions come together for challenge and inspiration, a place where we can help each other understand the mystery that lies at the heart of our existence.

SkyLight Paths sees both believers and seekers as a community that increasingly transcends traditional boundaries of religion and denomination—people wanting to learn from each other, *walking together, finding the way.*

SkyLight Paths, "Walking Together, Finding the Way" and colophon are trademarks of LongHill Partners, Inc. registered in the U.S. Patent and Trademark Office.

Walking Together, Finding the Way
Published by SkyLight Paths Publishing
A Division of LongHill Partners, Inc.
Sunset Farm Offices, Route 4, P.O. Box 237
Woodstock, VT 05091
Tel: (802) 457-4000   Fax: (802) 457-4004
www.skylightpaths.com

To every person
who had something hard to say
and said it.

Contents

Preface

I hope this book will bring joy to your lips, clarity to your words, and the partnership of the holy in hard times. Here we have a small permission to enter difficulty with hope: We don't have to be afraid that we don't know what to say. We can say what we need to say, without fear, in love, knowing that the truth is beautiful and that the Spirit is with us. This guide puts legs under that truth: It teaches us how to use sacred speech.

Introduction: Sacred Speech in the Glocal World

"O Lord, open thou my lips and let my mouth show forth thy praise."

—*Psalm 51:15*

Sacred speech is speech plus Spirit. Speech without Spirit is just speech; speech with Spirit acknowledged becomes sacred. The action of changing ordinary speech into sacred speech is as simple as opening a door: We walk into a new room and there Spirit is with us. Sacred speech opens doors and takes risks. The markers of sacred speech are:

- An acknowledgment of the presence of God in the words we use,
- A maximization of the possibility of love and caring,
- A minimization of fear.
- Linkage, connection, contact: Sacred speech bridges divides.

Sacred speech affirms and grounds us; it also inspires and shakes us up. Sacred speech is multidimensional and lives intentionally in a multidimensional world. Sacred speech is not just lateral, between one human being and another. Sacred speech assumes a third partner, the Spirit, who carries on wings what we utter in voice. Sacred speech is not just horizontal, but horizontal and vertical simultaneously. It is grounded and winged, air and earth, *chronos* and *kairos*. Because the criteria for sacred speech are spiritual—because we open doors and take risks by a borrowed and learned power not wholly our own—sacred speech is less teachable than it is learnable. I can show the way, but not everyone can walk or talk the way. Many can go to the threshold, but not everyone can cross it. I can give concrete examples, then hope that the Spirit will breathe the sacred part into our breath and our use of it. Here I point many ways to sacred speech—to the art and act of sacred speaking—and assume the Spirit will do the rest.

Speech that is not sacred is not just secular and not just one-dimensional. Nor is sacred speech the ketchup we put on the hamburger or the parsley we put on the plate; it is not an addition. It is not something we do to add flavor or color or to make things look good. Instead, sacred speech is part of the whole of speech and, therefore, not divisible into "holy" and "unholy," "sacred" and "profane." Secular speech ignores Spirit and tends to close doors and keep people "safe"—so safe, in fact, that they are in great danger of missing out on life. Sacred speech can talk about ketchup in a way that recognizes Spirit.

The American poet James Galvin points to this essentially spiritual dilemma when he says, "Religion is a noose around my neck—and it keeps me from hanging." We want our words to make us safe and we want our words to make us free—and both are possible when we learn the art of sacred speech.

Sacer and *profanus* have long divided the world. Their meanings are not always easy to discern, as the two realms commingle with great regularity. Nevertheless, here I try to be a priest, or *sacerdos,* to words. Here I try to find the sacred part of words.

Religions of all kinds, especially the Abrahamic traditions and activist Buddhist groups, have always tried "to get a word in edge-wise" in the secular sphere. Ancient religions even have special language and rules regarding *lah-shon rah,* Hebrew for the sacred use of the tongue. There are dozens of rules against gossip, cruel wit, and telling a secret that is told to you. All these matters are small and regular and ordinary experiences of small, regular, ordinary human beings. We are mightily tempted to use our tongues, for good or for evil, about every ten minutes or so throughout our lives! Learning the holy use of the tongue, the art of sacred speech, is a holy endeavor.

The French philosopher Pascal declared that "nature is an infinite sphere whose center is everywhere, whose circumference is nowhere." There is no need to abandon the secular in order to speak in holy ways. Instead, there is a need to deepen the secular to its root dimension. Here we do not pit the secular against the sacred, or vice versa, so much as we let the ordinary develop and deepen into the extraordinary.

Louise Bogan, the American poet, argues that a certain method for stilling poetic talent is to substitute an outer battle for an inner one. Very often we keep our words shallow precisely to avoid the deep. This book is for those who are bored with the shallow and want to take the risk of the deep—for people who are not so much anti-secular as pro-spirit, for people who want to find the depth and multidimensionality of life.

This book speaks most directly to clergy and people of strong religious beliefs in many faiths and denominations. To say that it is only for the already religious, however, is to misunderstand sacred speech. Some of the most holy of speakers are without religious credential or portfolio. Indeed, learning the art of sacred speech can be a pathway for mature spirituality, especially for those who have found other pathways blocked and wanting. This book is for the spiritual "English major," someone who loves language and knows its power and wants also to love God.

Throughout this book, I use the words *God* and *Spirit* openly, as the God beyond God, the God beyond Christianity, Judaism, Islam, Buddhism, or *Star Trek*. I usually call this God "Spirit," as a way of being as inclusive as possible. I believe in one God who is beyond the claim of any and every name. As a Christian, I believe Jesus is a most excellent way to God but not the only excellent way to God.

The examples I use in this book are directed not just at speech that talks about Spirit but also at speech that carries Spirit in secular language. Most religious professionals and people committed to a faith will tell you that they are no strangers to the secular experience. Indeed, the most often asked questions I face as a religious professional involve interpreting the ordinary experiences of life (infidelity, broken hearts, joy, transcendence, accidents, transplant failures, serendipity, violence, bigotry, stupidity) in religious contexts. One morning my husband said to me, after he had delivered a fairly long lament about a distressing matter in his department at work, "You must go through this all the time!" I was pleased by his recognition of my reality. Like other clergy, I am rarely visited by people who are not in some kind of trouble. People don't just drop by to shoot the breeze with clergy. We are almost always approached by those experiencing difficulty. We learn the art of sacred speech precisely because we are honored by human difficulty. People want us to "say something." The same is true for most leaders in society. They are rarely approached with the simple matter. They are daily and regularly approached with complex matters. Thus, this book is written most directly for the spiritually developed person and for those who are helping people work toward that goal.

This book is a spiritual guide to using the holy gift of speech. It is "how to," grounded in a humble way of being, expressing an attitude of gratitude toward the tongue, in the knowledge that speech is a gift from God and we have a choice to use our mouths virtuously, in the most humble and searching sense of that word.

Sacred speech has clear markers, once it acknowledges God and establishes links between the sacred and secular spheres. One marker is the ability to love; another is a lessened tendency toward fear. We know something sacred is happening when love marks our speech and when fear does not. These are matters of degrees, not completion: We maximize love and minimize fear in sacred speech.

Holy speech is able to speak nonviolently, in love, as opposed to speaking in self-defense. When we speak in holy ways, our words have the capacity for love. We do not bring in the fight-or-flight response, in self-defense, but approach the loving use of speech in a different way, a way that opens doors and takes risks. Holy speech is not unprotected so much as it is protected more deeply in a larger love. There is a certain virginity to holy speech, an innocence that lets us reach for godlike capacity in the use of our speech.

Sacred speech is surely more a gift from God than a skill we can learn. It is a divine intention that can become a human intention.

Learning can advance us toward a more holy use of language. We can prepare ourselves and deepen our capacity for holy speech.

Especially now, as we live in a world where Babel is basic, where many languages are ordinary and confusion normal, we need a reorientation to the holy use of speech. In the Hebrew Scripture, Babel is the name of the tower around which the tribes stood and couldn't understand each other. As they gathered under the Tower of Babel, there is a hint that the people had not heard the multiplicity of language from all the clans before—and there they were, newly alert to the many tongues that constitute humanity. In the twenty-first century, we are once again newly aware of just how global the globe is. By gift of technology and travel, we know more about size and diversity than we have ever known before. We still live locally, with addresses, in homes, in nations, in cultures with individual tongues. Many of us also live globally, using more than one language per day and moving between time zones with alacrity. A new word, *glocal*, global and local, describes the complexity of our times.

Another clear mark of sacred speech is an ability to do "both/and," instead of "either/or," types of speaking and thinking. Sacred speech includes rather than excludes. Sacred speech links spheres. Many people fear that we can use only "politically correct" language once we understand diversity. In learning sacred speech, we overcome that fear. We learn how to do the right thing without having to be cynical about it.

Learning to open our mouths and let forth praise is something we learned as children and have to relearn again and again. We did learn how to talk in the local world; now we must relearn the art of speech in a glocal world. The world has changed much since we were young, and it will keep on changing. This book is about learning to speak, again and again, in a renewable, ongoing way in the glocal world.

Babel is basic—but that doesn't mean we can't understand each other or speak in godly ways to each other. Babble—the jumbled word that sounds a lot like Babel—is not necessary. Self-protection inside our "native" tongue is likewise not necessary. Instead, we can find our way to the experience that came to those under the ancient Tower of Babel. They experienced a miracle: They glimpsed what it meant to understand each other. The holy use of the tongue is possible tribally and post-tribally. The sacred art of speech is possible in our cultural home as well as in our global home. In the new century, love hasn't gone out of style, nor has the need to find a path beyond fear.

1

To Be Humble

Sacred speech is about God more than it is about human beings. Sacred speech knows we live in a vertical, not a horizontal, world and that God's presence or Spirit in our words is possible. Sacred speech, therefore, maximizes love and minimizes fear. It also unites what is divided. It lives through the double bind, beyond the world of either/or, into the world of both/and.

A singular characteristic of sacred speech is its openness. It is humble. It is less interested in being right than in being linked, less interested in self-protection than in self-expression, less interested in cages and doors than in decks and windows. Sacred speech wants clarity and it wants justice. Sacred speech loves a good, honest boundary. But it also wants to maximize love and minimize fear. Sacred speech understands and acknowledges that, in the world God has made, we need not fear. We may require many fewer locks and keys, borders, and boundaries than we think we do.

Examples of sacred speech can be found throughout our daily lives, at home and at work. In this book, I've recounted instances in which people have given themselves space for sacred speech, such as this encounter between a boss and his assistant.

Speech That Carries Spirit

The manager stormed into his assistant's cubicle. His body was already speaking. The message was anger. The assistant had seen this behavior before. She started counting inside, from one to thirty, before the manager said a word. "Why are there so many typos in this memo?" "Because I had to get it out on very short notice," she said quietly, after she had kept her peace until the number thirty arrived. Then she stayed silent and, oddly, he stayed silent too. The quietness of her response had evoked a quiet in him. In the silence, something akin to understanding was beginning. Both people had made a mistake. The quietness of the assistant's excuse was still making its point when she continued, "I'd really like to produce better work. How can we make that happen?"

Differing levels of status are often the beginning of communication problems. We can even the playing field by asserting ourselves quietly. The Tower of Babel story that I mentioned in the introduction is not just about many languages but also about the many levels of human beings. The wrong question to ask in the glocal world is, "How can I stay on top?" The right question to ask is, "How can we find ways to 'just get along'?" as Rodney King's famous plea did. Imagine the previous story in a more "hyphenated" context: The assistant is African-American; the boss is Asian-American. Imagine any simple interaction made more complex by any version of the hyphens—and then add the ordinary confusions of race, ethnicity, and nationality, and you begin to see why sacred speech is so important. It is our only way to find the "bless in the mess" of mature, twenty-first-century living. Religious leaders are asked the "right" way to think about such matters a hundred times a day: What do we do when the boss yells at us? This book is a guide to what to do when we are in a mess and want to find the blessing in and through it. Humility is the key.

Humility is not self-abasement. Nor is humility the incapacity to defend ourselves or to hold our ground. Instead, humility is a reaching toward the other, even when the other is being unfair. Humility is humility before God: We hold our ground quietly, as the assistant did, because we know God is with us. We don't need to win the battle to know that we are okay. First, we know that we are okay—and then we are able to enter battles without desperation to win.

This freedom in Spirited living is well expressed in one of William Sloane Coffin Jr.'s oft-repeated aphorisms: "I'm not okay and you're not okay and that's okay." This phrase says why we are humble. We know we are not on earth to become okay. We already are God's creatures and, therefore, we are okay. We do our best to do our job. We are not defined by what we do at our job or by what someone else thinks we have or have not done. Indeed, praise is as much a culprit as blame: Either way, an "outsider" is in charge of our state of mind. Most of us hate to be criticized and love to be praised. Either way, though, we are living too deeply in the horizontal world and insufficiently in the vertical world, the one where Spirit matters. Either way, we are letting small matters tell us who we are.

A great deal of miscommunication and misinformation happens because the people who are conversing lack spiritual humility. They want to walk away justified, redeemed, made right and whole by the other. This form of self-justification is unjustified. If Spirit is real, Spirit justifies—not our boss or spouse, our résumé, or anything else.

When we look deeply at the Tower of Babel story and the Pentecost story, which is the parallel in Christian Scripture, we find two ancient tales of language commanding a sacred use across borders and boundaries of all kinds. We find that self-justification and national justification have caused people trouble for a long time. In the Pentecost story, fire lights on the heads of Jesus' disciples and they find a way to hear each other, even though they all speak different languages. They speak in "tongues," widely understood not just to be glossalia in its ecstatic dimension but also to be linguistic understanding. Both at Babel and in the upper room on Pentecost (told in Acts 2:1–12), people find a way to understand one another. They are filled with the Holy Spirit, and that is the prelude to genuine, almost miraculous communication as well as to "just getting along."

An old joke helps. "What is a trilinguist? One who speaks three languages. What is a bilinguist? One who speaks two languages. What is a monolinguist? An American." More powerful nations often get other people to speak their language rather than learning the tongue of the "other." English is probably the one language that can "unBabel" the world for *you*. Those who want to use their tongues in a holy way want to speak as God would speak. God speaks in more than one language, and there is little evidence that English is the language of Heaven. God is intentionally multicultural and, therefore, intentionally multilingual.

To speak sacredly, we become multilingual, even if we speak only one language. We acknowledge diversity at its and our depths, as origin, alpha and omega. We learn to speak glocally. I don't mean so much becoming multilingual as speaking one language fully conscious that there is more than one language. We approach the virtue of divine seeing, that we are wonderful but not total, that we are particular but not all, that we are so much protected that we need not protect ourselves.

Sacred speech is not just speech about Spirit. It is speech that carries Spirit to a miraculous multilingual state of being. We understand each other. We don't even know how. Bosses understand administrative assistants and assistants understand bosses!

We who are professional religious people spend less of our time telling people about God than we do telling them how to remember God in ordinary circumstances. Sacred speech remembers God in ordinary circumstances. Sacred speech is divinely secured—and delivered on earth. In the glocal world, we secure each other by understanding each other's speech, the way God intended.

Speech That Carries Spirit

A woman was applying for a job. Her native language was Spanish, her second language English. In her former country, she was a medical doctor. Her specialty was neurology. In the United States, she had no standing with the medical community, and thus she was applying for a job as a technician in a neurologist's office. The neurologist interviewing her was concerned that she was overqualified. "Would you announce diagnoses to patients before I had a chance to review the tests? Would you read the tests and let people know what they showed, say, about carpal tunnel syndrome?" She responded, "Yes, I would probably make that mistake if I knew how to say 'carpal tunnel syndrome' in English." She said "carpal tunnel syndrome" in Spanish—or so the neurologist thought, because he didn't know much Spanish, just the way she didn't know much English. Her humor deflected what might have become a power struggle. She also told the truth: She would be jealous because of her status and knowledge. She got the job.

Sacred speech combines local autonomy and language with global deference and respect. Sacred speech understands what it is like to be a medical doctor in one country and a technician in another. Sacred speech understands levels but rarely approves them. It links levels so that people can find each other across borders and boundaries. Spiritually mature people and religious professionals teach people how to link; that is one of our main functions.

Kofi Annan, winner of the Nobel Peace Prize and Secretary General of the United Nations, says that when he first went to St. Paul, Minnesota, to attend Macalester College, he thought earmuffs were a very silly piece of clothing. He was a child of the Tropics; he had never been out of the Southern Hemisphere. "Only when I returned from a brisk winter walk with my ears frozen did I have to conclude that the natives probably knew what they were doing. This was an early lesson that Macalester taught me: Never walk into an environment and assume that you understand it better than the people who live there."[1]

He also speaks of courage: "Courage does not mean the lack of fear but rather the ability to overcome fear." Sacred speech takes risks that move us beyond the awesome fear of not being able to understand one another. If we cannot understand each other, war is inevitable and injustice is the name of our home. If we can understand each other—without having to give up our tribe, our native land, even some of our nationalism—we have a chance at peace and a hope for justice. Sacred speech is learning to talk the way God talks. Sacred speech is learning to think the way God thinks. Sacred speech stands under the Tower of Babel without babbling. It does not idolize and become God in order to be holy: The act of holy speaking is a humble—not proud—activity, even though it is Godlike.

Sacred speech imitates God's speech to humanity; it opens doors and takes risks in loving. It has both an ethnic and a cultural home and a universal perspective. Note the "both/and." We are able to be both African- or German-Americans and creatures of a loving God. We are universal and unique at the same time, not ghettoized and not taken away from the kind of food we like to eat, not forced out of our own culture. God made us that way.

Although sacred speech is a gift, not a skill, we can prepare ourselves to be more open to the gift. An old Zen Buddhist story shows the way. "Why," said the student to the master, "would I attend to

> Sacred speech has at least the following qualities. It opens doors because it is not afraid to open them. It takes risks because it is not afraid of the "other," even the "other" who speaks another way. It contains more love than fear. It is neither fight nor flight, the normal modes of self-defense. Instead, it is aware of its protection as a creature of God and has plenty of boundaries, sufficient to habituate love as behavior. Even though sacred speech is good and virtuous—the more classical way to express goodness—it is not proud. It is creaturely. The sacred art of speech is less a big thing than it is a good thing. Its key is humility.

all these spiritual disciplines if they don't guarantee me the gate of God?" "Because," the master reminded him, "they don't guarantee or manipulate God so much as make sure you are awake if God happens to pass by."

Spiritual self-help books have to be careful not to manipulate God or gift while simultaneously offering practical advice on how to prepare ourselves for virtue, expressed here in only one of its many facets, as the holy use of the tongue. Spiritual gifts are nothing if they are not humble. They stand small before the magnificence and largeness of God.

How can we tell whether our tongue is observant of the Spirit? By whether or not we are self-justifying, that awful defensive repeating over and over of how right we are and were and ever shall be. By letting go of being right and taking hold of God's manifold gifts of security and Spirit. When we switch our mouths from the closed gates of self-defense to the open gates of praise, we find ourselves able to communicate across boundaries, through levels and classes and stratifications of human beings. Every now and then, we experience the Tower of Babel and say, with utter awe, "I understood what that stranger said. I really understood. I got out of my own way, let Spirit carry me across the divide, and I really understood."

2

To Forgive

If you have ever been forgiven, you know just how holy an experience it is. Doors that were closed, relationships that were ended, paths that were cut off suddenly face a clearing instead of darkness. We can go on. Very often, the words carry the clearing to us and us to the clearing.

Often it is not the "other" who is forgiving us so much as God who is forgiving us. God provides the energy. Sacred speech comes from our center in God and reaches for the center in others. It pays more attention to the vertical, the alpha, the omega, the source, and the important than it does to our horizontal relationships with each other. Sacred speech happens horizontally but is based vertically. It considers the urgent but stays centered in the important. Sacred speech makes choices about what matters and has as its chief antagonist the trivial. Sometimes even large things, such as an extramarital affair, for example, are small in the larger scheme of things.

Speech That Carries Spirit

"I know I said I would never forgive you for having that affair. I know I said I never could forgive you. But the idea of going on in life without you is more than I can bear. We have children; they still love you. Thus I am forced, by the grace and power of God, to accept your apology and to trust that you won't go in that direction again. I speak not from my own power because alone I could never forgive you. Because God still loves you, I am going to try again."

We do not use speech to defend ourselves so much as we use it to open ourselves. "I" speech becomes safe. "I" can tell you I love you, treasure you, want to know you, and am disturbed by something you said. I have the permission and the commandment to enter difficulty with you in hope. I can open up things you might prefer to have closed. I know how to forgive—not by my power but by Spirit's power. Instead of "staying strong and firm," we become soft and vulnerable. That tenderness touches the tender part of others; we come out of the forest into a clearing. We can start again. No, we will never be the same. Some trust will disappear. Some scars will take a long time to scab over. But scabs beat walking around with an open wound, a wound that only festers over time.

"The great irony of trust is that in order to rebuild it, one must take risks with the person who broke it," says Professor Robert

Folger in an article on social psychology in the *Chronicle of Higher Education*. "You're trying to rebuild trust out of distrust . . . part of the way you would do that would be to be vulnerable. It's tricky. You hate an enemy that you've feuded with for generations. Your first step has to be tiny. That's the fine line. You can't afford to get your throat cut." Folger argues that such tiny steps are particularly hard in places of great conflict, such as the Middle East, because people have been trying confidence-building measures there for a long time. "You try doing stitches," he says, "then over the past 18 months, 10 years of stitching together was ripped out. Once it's ripped out, it takes 10 years to make up."[1]

Speech That Carries Spirit

The barber said to his long-term client, "Those Palestinians are acting like animals. Do you see the way they terrorize and commit suicide just to keep Israel on high alert all the time?" The client excused himself from the barber's chair and said he would have to come back later. He returned the next day and said in a quiet voice, "I am very disturbed to hear anyone speak of anyone as an animal. It reminds me of what happened to the Jews under Hitler, when they were robbed of their humanity." And then he waited. His barber said, "I am sorry. I understand. I'm upset too. But let's not let it get in the way of our relationship. There is enough damage already done."

It is so hard to speak of such "red flag" situations that most of us simply don't ever try. These two men tried—and after their frustration subsided, found each other. They found each other without avoiding the red flag and without shutting down. They preserved their relationship.

Psalm 90 is probably my favorite psalm. Basically the psalm says, "Life is short, so get wise soon." Getting wise late doesn't help you—and thus that marvelous transition phrase between the strophes of the psalm: "O satisfy us early with thy mercy so that we may be glad all our days." And, "So teach us to number our days that we may apply our hearts early to wisdom." Early wisdom, early mercy: Sacred speech gets to the words of forgiveness as quickly as it can after something bad happens.

People who want to learn sacred speech often memorize psalms or parts of psalms. They are a part of Hebrew Scripture, also prayed by Christians. We teach ourselves to get to the words of mercy quickly by such memory. Listen to Psalm 90:

Lord, you have been our dwelling place in all generations. Before the mountains were brought forth, or ever you had formed the earth and the world, from everlasting to everlasting you are God. You turn us back to dust, and say, "Turn back, you mortals." For a thousand years in your sight are like yesterday when it is past, or like a watch in the night. You sweep them away; they are like a dream, like grass that is renewed in the morning; in the morning it flourishes and is renewed; in the evening it fades and withers. For we are consumed by your anger; by your wrath we are overwhelmed. You have set our iniquities before you, our secret sins in the light of your countenance. For all our days pass away under your wrath; our years come to an end like a sigh. The days of our life are seventy years, or perhaps eighty, if we are strong; even then their span is only toil and trouble; they are soon gone, and we fly away. Who considers the power of your anger? Your wrath is as great as the fear that is due you. So teach us to count our days that we may gain a wise heart. Turn, O Lord! How long? Have compassion on your servants! Satisfy us in the morning with your steadfast love, so that we may rejoice and be glad all our days. Make us glad as many days as you have afflicted us, and as many years as we have seen evil. Let your work be manifest to your servants, and your glorious power to their children. Let the favor of the Lord our God be upon us, and prosper for us the work of our hands—O prosper the work of our hands!

Forgiveness can happen early or late—when we realize just how short life is, we usually want it to happen early. We want to know how to have the goal of perpetual forgiveness already in our hearts; then the right words come. Instead of saying, "I could never forgive you for that," we say, "I will be able to forgive you but not just yet."

Some people can forgive their enemies and some cannot. Some people can forgive their parents for what they did or didn't do—and some cannot. Some cannot forgive the world's terrorists. Many live a foot away from forgiveness but can't quite break down into it. Melting in forgiveness means going forward into a new world, in a new way. Most of us aren't very good at it.

That's why Jesus' admonition that we forgive debt—even monetary debts—with grace and wit and gladness is more than a little difficult. We know he is right, but we don't know how to be like him. Jesus argues that forgiving an unpaid debt is better than living without forgiveness.

Let me tell you a story from *Far Above Rubies,* a novel by Cynthia Polansky. It is a story of someone going farther than she had to—for someone she really didn't know and who wasn't really like her. Her example teaches us what it takes to genuinely forgive a debt.

We have to go further than we know how to go. And we have to go one step at a time.

Certainly, Polansky doesn't turn the tragedy of the Holocaust into romance or comedy in her book, but she does tame it. She tells the story of a woman in Amsterdam, "Tante Soof," or Sofie, who marries a Jew and adopts his six daughters. Her mother tells her she is making a serious mistake—about the man, about the family, and about her own prospects. Sofie marries Jan anyway and not only adopts his children but also falls in love with them, so much so that when their names appear on the list to go to the work camps, she makes a rather abrupt decision to go with them. Her name is not on the list. Still, she makes the journey with them, as defiantly as when she first married Jan. Her departure from Jan is portrayed with an artistic accuracy that leaves the reader sure that Sofie's story can only improve. "What else can I do? . . . they are my daughters. They cannot go alone. . . ."

Polansky then gives us a composite of camp life, detail by detail, borrowing from many factual stories to compose a fictional account of what happens to the girls and their stepmother. The sexual abuse, the failed rebellions against the guards, the lack of food, the inadequate clothing, the fear to use the toilet, the work, the bosom-hidden letters, the determination about whether to sell a precious stone ring or keep it for later protection, the chapped lips and broken fingernails—all these details of oppression are carefully developed by the author to give a picture of heroism chapter by chapter.

Separation follows separation in the work camp stories. Every Monday, a list is posted in the "dining" hall to indicate who is going to the next hellhole and who is staying behind. A moment of tragedy occurs when, one Monday, all seven of the women are on the same list. They are all going to a death camp. They actually rejoice. "Sofie couldn't decide which was worse, the loneliness of unspoken fears or the despair of shared ones."

In the end, Sofie survives the camps. The daughters do and don't make it in their own ways—readers will have to find out for themselves. But the story of courage that composes this and the other tales grafted upon it keeps the reader turning the pages very rapidly. Sofie is not portrayed as a saint so much as a survivor: Everything she does is not perfect. She is survived by her niece, the author Cynthia Polansky, and can be "adopted" by those whose own destinies are unremarked and unremembered.

Many people don't know what happened to their forebears. Sofie lives in that kind of treacherous ignorance long after she survives one form of death. She does more than forgive the Nazis: She transcends them and belittles them in that transcendence. Based on the proverb, "A woman of valor who can find? For her price is far above rubies," this book doesn't make the Holocaust palatable, but it honors the witnesses by telling the story.[2]

Those of us who want to know sacred speech and who want to be wise can find a model in Sofie. She did what she didn't think she could do. She did it because, as she says, "What else can I do?" That is the source of most genuine forgiveness.

What do we get from hanging on to our debts? Not much. The only result is separation from those whom we could love.

It is possible that forgiveness is a form of the highest pragmatism. No, we don't always survive something as horrific as the death camps. Or the trouble of someone who has deeply hurt us. Or stolen from us. Or beat us. Or raped us. Or done something "unforgivable." But still, what do we get out of hanging on to the debt? When we let the debt go, we lean toward God. We do what we can't do. And God does the rest. God makes our speech sacred by doing what we think we can't do.

What is wisdom? Apparently, according to Psalm 90, wisdom is mercy. Or at least a large part of wisdom is the capacity to have mercy. Thus, people who can't be merciful toward themselves about their own need for antacid pills or vision tests probably can't have much mercy toward others. Wisdom means being merciful toward yourself as your life changes.

Surely wisdom is not merciless. What wise nation would spend $80,000 per year to incarcerate a juvenile offender instead of $30,000 to give him a college education? What wise nation would keep a person convicted of a drug arrest ineligible for financial aid for a college education? Has anyone noticed the federal financial aid form for colleges lately? It says, "Have you ever been convicted of possession or selling illegal drugs? If you have, answer 'Yes.' Complete and submit this application and we will send you a worksheet in the mail for you to determine if your conviction affects your eligibility for aid. Do not leave question 35 blank."

In 2001, forty-seven thousand of the ten million applicants for federal student aid lost eligibility for some or all of their assistance because of past drug convictions or because they failed to answer a question about drug use on the application. Of those forty-seven thousand, more than 60 percent lost financial aid for the entire year; 20 percent left the question blank and did not get any aid; and a little under 20 percent lost financial aid for part of the year. Why do these figures matter? Because they are merciless. Because they aren't wise. Because they put kids already in trouble into more trouble. Because they are based in punishment rather than in mercy. Questions like Number 35 are the opposite of sacred speech: They close doors and create fear. They are not wise.

No, I am not condoning (listen for the punitive language) or recommending light penalties for drug use. But I know a young man named John who would like to be a student at a local community college. He did do drugs in high school; he spent one night in jail and was fined a hundred dollars for possession of marijuana when he was sixteen. He doesn't do drugs anymore. He is twenty-three. He worked for two years and now wants to get a degree. He received a letter from the education department saying that he would not be eligible for student aid because of a previous drug conviction. Now he will have to drop out of school and get a job. What do you really think will happen to John because of this punishment for his crime? Will John contribute to society all that he could? Or will John be just another wasted talent, someone who took a stupid risk and has to pay too long for it? If we are lucky, John will find a wise person to help him through his anger, his resentment, his guilt, his trouble. That person will know mercy. If we are not lucky, John will go back to drugs. He may even rob you to get them.

Forgiveness may be the highest pragmatism as well as something very, very holy.

In my experience, people also have difficulties with punishments that do not "fit the crime." Sabotage of a career, for instance, is not appropriate punishment for a stupid practical joke played by a drunken conventioneer who should have known better but didn't. But how do we know? And when is it as unwise not to punish as it is to punish? Even in our otherwise perfect family (ha!), things have happened to test us. An incident last fall involved my teenage son borrowing the car and driving it when his name was not on the insurance policy. He knew that was the case, and, of course, he had a fender bender that evening while driving six of his friends to hear Ralph

Nader speak. He thought his destination would pacify me. It did not. He not only had a fender bender, but he also ran into a man whose middle name, apparently, was Litigious. For several months we awaited the astronomical repair bill that was surely coming. It never arrived. Should we wisely assume that was sufficient punishment for our darling? I thought not. A larger consequence than just "getting lucky and getting off" should prevail. Thus, this child of mine got the car keys back on June 1 and not sooner.

Don't confuse mercy with wisdom. Sometimes mercy means punishment. Sometimes appropriate punishment can prevent future drug use, car key stealing, and midnight pranks. Appropriate punishment can be wise. Inappropriate punishment, on the other hand, is rarely wise.

How do we apply these principles to the risks we have to manage? How do we keep ourselves from shooting ourselves in the foot, so to speak, while aiming at a terrorist or an addict? How do we use punishment in a sacred way, a way that eventually winds down the road to forgiveness and reconciliation? How do we keep ourselves from protecting democracy through undemocratic means, making peace by waging war, sending kids to jail to learn how to be better criminals? How do we let wisdom temper punishment so that mercy will prevail?

Surely we start with Representative Mark Souder of Indiana, the author of the drug law, who says its application has been much more severe nationwide than he intended. He has since made attempts to correct the law. That is mercy in action, and we can commend him.

We also learn to do what he is doing. We can learn the fine art of saying, "Whoops, I made a mistake." We become merciful toward ourselves. That is the basis for mercy for others. Indeed, forgiveness is not something that we direct only toward others. The art of sacred speech in the matter of forgiveness has to do with being ready to admit mistakes, to say we are wrong, to say "whoops" and mean it. Saying "whoops" is sacred speech.

I have made so many parenting mistakes in my life that I consider myself an expert at parenting. I have even had to apologize to my children. For example, once I phoned a high school drama teacher and blessed him out for not casting my daughter in one of the lead roles. How could he not have seen her

Forgiveness happens when people stay in the "I" and don't get lost in the "you" or the accusation. Forgiveness comes from God. We simply carry it to each other on behalf of love, on behalf of going on and not getting stuck in the rut of hate and hurt. Forgiveness is the highest form of pragmatism, because it opens doors that lingering hurt will surely close.

Two Zen Buddhist masters were climbing down the hill from a terrible prison where they had been beaten and tortured. They were finally free. One said to the other, "I have forgiven them for what they did to me." The other said, "I will never forgive them, never, never, never." The first said, "So they still have you in jail, right?"

brilliance and her talent? She had auditioned for only the two lead roles and had spent weeks imagining herself as a great actress. He then cast her in one of the minor roles. She took to her bed. Being an ordinary parent—that is, one who cannot tolerate a child's grief whatsoever—I called the director and tried not to be like those other people, the ones who demand favors for their children. I merely suggested a change in his pedagogy, with rage deep in my heart and voice. "Why not try her out for a *minor* part, if that's all you're going to give her? Why elevate her expectations only to dash them?" He was no slouch in the anger department either, and he told me he was triple-casting the play, working very hard, and didn't need my guff. After that mistake, I compounded it by telling my daughter how I had defended her honor. She went back to bed and didn't speak to me for two solid days, something that had never happened before in our relationship. Things got worse until I realized that I had taken one suffering (not getting the part) and turned it into a much bigger mess than it was. Instead of applying the wisdom of restraint and companionship in suffering, I had applied the stupidity of control and anger.

By coincidence, the girl chosen for the lead role was deported. My daughter got the part and I got the wisdom. The price of the wisdom was two apologies, one to the drama teacher and one to my daughter.

Control is rarely wisdom. Companionship and participation are often wisdom. Hanging in with somebody is almost always wisdom. It is also merciful. Thus, a proper reading of Psalm 90 would tell us to hang in with kids who take stupid risks, such as using drugs. When our very short lives are over, we can hope to stand on the merciful, not punitive, side of the ledger. "Teach us, O God, an early wisdom." Life is short—get wise early.

Sacred speech as forgiveness often means a good healthy connection to the word "I." "I am sorry. I forgive you." The whole person comes along in big sentences like that. In holy intimacy, I avoid "you" conversation. I don't say, "You are really bugging me." Or "You should never have had that affair in the first place." Instead I say, "I am really bothered or hurt by what you just said." Therapists speak about staying in the "I." When we know the grace of God that makes even the approval of our closest partner appropriately penultimate, we are able to stay in the "I." When we get scared, we start the "you" talk.

Religious professionals and spiritual people have an obligation to teach "I" talk at both the deepest and the most trivial levels. We incarnate sacred speech. We help people make it real in their ordinary lives.

Speech That Carries Spirit

"You are driving me crazy . . . with that turning of the page while I am trying to sleep."

"I'm sorry, darling, I will go read on the couch—but I really want to stay close to you."

Notice the absence of defense: "I can read my paper if I want to. . . ."

Notice the absence of advice: "No one can drive you crazy unless you let them."

Notice the absence of excuses: "You say I am bugging you and I agree with you."

Notice the moving closer while the other is distancing.

Notice that an apology always goes a long way to defuse a tense situation.

Fear causes us to think that if we lose our lover's or best friend's approval we are finished, wiped out, destroyed. Sacred speech knows that no person can destroy us and that nothing can separate us from the love of God. Those who are capable of the most intimacy are those who are most centered—and therefore freer to take the most risks. Saying "I'm sorry" matters terribly to those who have little center. We slip into nothingness when we have done wrong. Saying "I'm sorry" as a centered person is a loss of almost nothing.

When confronted with difficult issues, the best thing intimates can learn to do is ask questions. A good one is, "Could you tell me more?" We urge the other to self-disclose; we don't expose or "uncloset" him or her. Especially if we are disturbed by something he or she is saying (or not saying), we need the simple tool of "tell me more." That phrase all by itself is godly. It means we are interested. It means we are ready. It means we want to know. It imitates the relationship God has with humanity—where we are always urged to tell God more about who we are and where we are stuck. It is also the sentence that best walks the path to forgiveness. Instead of trying to find out who is right and who is wrong—a dead end and an unspiritual act of the highest order—we agree to listen. "Tell me more."

Speech That Carries Spirit

"I wish our relationship had more excitement. . . ."

"Tell me more . . . about what you want. . . ."

"I want to see more plays, make love more, go for long walks, have a sense that you really know me, through and through. . . ."

"Tell me more. . . ."

"I want to linger over dinner and laugh. I want you to think I'm the best-looking person you ever met. . . ."

"Tell me more. . . ."

Notice the refusal to defend. Most people hear the need for more excitement as a straight-out accusation. "What, didn't we have lots of excitement just last week . . . and what about that trip last summer?"

Notice the absence of self-justification.

Notice the genuine interest in hearing.

"Tell me more" is a way of granting the request for connection, which is what just about any complaint in any relationship really is. Such a strategy also means that we have in our spiritual pocket an alternative to control. We learn these alternatives by living, by memorizing psalms, by studying Scripture, by being pragmatic about life at the highest level. "Don't tell me that" is the opposite of "Tell me more." Many of us shut down to our intimates without even knowing it because we don't want to hear what they are really saying. Many a partner stops being able to hear a loved one because he or she has begun to express unhappiness most of the time. We stop listening when we don't want to hear what the other has to say. When we don't hear what the other has to say, we also don't respond or speak well.

Sacred speech self-differentiates; it speaks plainly and personally and directly. It keeps good boundaries on behalf of good relationships. Intimates use "I" language because it is fundamentally secure. No human can secure us. But Spirit and Source sufficiently secure us for relationships that are fair and just and caring. We develop into people who can use the "I" word well: "I, who am a real person with real capacity and realization of who I am, forgive you." "I, who am a real person with real capacity and realization of who I am, am sorry." Sacred speech sets limits *and* tests boundaries: It is free to do both.

Out of our security, we are able to forgive. We are able to go on. We are able to do things that we, alone, "can't do." Spirit does them through us. Spirit keeps the air and water circulating in a relationship by a nearly constant process of forgiveness.

In public, as well as in intimate life, forgiveness is an important art. Those who have been oppressed by racism or sexism or homophobia are also in great need of the art of forgiveness. Otherwise, they internalize the oppressor's power.

Speech That Carries Spirit
"I know I didn't get the job because I am gay. They couldn't say it out loud, but I know how they think. I know where they go to church and I heard what that preacher said about my sinfulness. I have a couple of choices. I can sue them. I can also go on and find another job. I can even pray for them. I wonder how many more years it will take before people understand. It took African-Americans almost three hundred years. . . . I guess I can wait a little longer."

By the way, it may also at times be holy and sacred to litigate. But when oppression is the norm, we need other arrows in our quiver than mere justice. God defends us with anger and with relief from anger.

Sacred speech opens doors, even when the gates of oppression are locked. It does so by letting us take the next step, to "go on" and not get stuck in anger or fear or depression. Sacred speech clears away the confusion and creates futures for people who think they have none. Sacred speech maximizes love, minimizes fear, and creates the links that let people move toward each other and toward God.

3

To Praise

When Spirit is a part of our life, we spend most of our time in praise. We find our way to the good. We speak of it. We are not "optimistic" so much as joyful. We know that God is up to good in the world and that knowledge bubbles over in speech.

TO PRAISE THE WORLD

Many of us spend the day going to meetings or in conversations that are of the "tsk, tsk, ain't it awful" variety. One recent evening, I spent three hours listening to a forum about Florida's political despair. My dinner companions were worried to pieces about the redistricting of congressional districts. Their fear was well founded; their party stood to lose quite a bit and not just for a short time but for a long time. But even something this difficult can be placed in a larger context of praise.

Sacred speech does lament; it can even complain and mouth words of despair. But it doesn't stay there. It doesn't get stuck in lament. Sacred speech finds its way to praise the world underneath the world that seems to be. Sacred speech understands that "weeping may linger for the night but joy comes in the morning," as Psalm 30:5 puts it. Sacred speech understands, as Martin Luther King Jr. did, that God is in charge of history, not human beings. Thus, we may use words to announce our grief and disappointment, but we do so in a way that returns to praise as soon as possible. We do what we can about redistricting (or failures to let voting be fair) and we remember that God is in charge. God, not human folly or evil, will win in the end.

I think of the way in which many African-American churches use the chant, "God is good all the time." They actually mean something quite complex. They mean that everything, even the bad part, is always working together for good. Those of us who have suffered often have a hard time believing this truth under the truth of trouble. We have lost a sacred capacity, the capacity to praise the world as it is while praising the world for what it will yet be.

Praise is the opposite of complaint. It seeks the river of joy beyond the rivulets of pessimism. Praise is not a form of speech that denies pessimism; for all I know, my companions at the dinner were right. Political reapportionment may be a trial for many years to come. But even that level of institutionalizing injustice does not mean that Spirit is not to be praised. Spirit finds a way. Spirit comes through for us. You have only to know a terminally ill person who wakes up every morning with joy in his heart to know what I mean.

There are, by the way, many of these joyful people. Hospice workers are constantly telling stories of people who treasure their last days and their last breaths.

One of the key trials in our rapidly changing world is that many people refuse to praise it. Instead they bemoan it. The implication in the nostalgic idea that the good old days were so much better is that Spirit is also dead, or at least retired. Those who know Spirit in speech and in life know that Spirit is alive.

There is an odd pragmatism to sacred speech. Even for those who doubt the vitality of Spirit, there are reasons to praise the world as it is. Doris Sommer, a professor of Romance languages and literature at Harvard, argues that "inherited tastes and dispositions have become obstacles to democratic life." What we get from enjoying diversity is access to "an international code that could foster communication, commerce and creativity." These are not small prizes. She says that a cultivated response to linguistic differences "would be to do a double take; it would be to feel fear and enjoy the pleasure of reflecting on that fear." The *Chronicle of Higher Education* titled this small piece of pro-diversity education "Speaking in Tongues."[1]

One real challenge in the contemporary world is the challenge of diversity. Many people praise diversity only to become afraid of it in actual communal practice. Those who know the sacred speech of praise describe the wonderful problem of multicultural speech in a maturing world. Sacred speech praises the new world—without being Pollyannaish about the challenges of diversity and "babble." The old-fashioned religious word for praise is *witness:* We speak of what we see deep down. We speak of what we see of Spirit's action in the world. We do see trouble, but we also see below trouble and through trouble.

One wonderful definition of a godly person is that he or she enters difficulty with hope. We are invited to enter difficulty with hope and we are commanded to enter difficulty with hope by most of our ancient religious traditions. Thus, we praise the challenge of diversity precisely because it is difficult. We avoid the nostalgia and the "tsks" in praising the world as it is. By that praise, we learn to love it.

WHAT IS SACRED
IN MULTICULTURAL SPEECH

As we make the transition to a more transparently multicultural world, we find ourselves easily making mistakes. The world has always been multicultural; now we know just how many cultures there are. Now we bump into each other more frequently and thus need words to speak to one another. Here in Miami, I often wonder whether people prefer to be called black or African-American, Hispanic or Latino, young woman or girl, young man or boy. I find myself using all these words and more in public speech so as not to offend anyone or create the illusion of exclusion. Exclusion is often an illusion, because no one really has the power to exclude another, try as we might, intentionally or unintentionally. Still, I am very careful with my speech in public. Some of us choose care because we don't want to be exclusive; others just want to avoid trouble or comment. There are truly gorgeous advantages in public multicultural speech that is joyfully spoken. There is great joy in learning how to do it well and in addressing the sacred nature of the issue.

What is holy about multicultural speech is that it uses words to acknowledge God's creation, which was in the very beginning a decision for difference, a choice for many cultures, not one. In other words, multi is the norm. Tribal is not the norm. Multicultural is the matured. Making the shift from seeing the world in our way to seeing it in God's way is the first step in making public speech holy. When we praise the goodness of the maturing world, we don't just surprise people. We engage them. In the context of something positive, we can take many risks. If the initiating context is already negative, it becomes very hard to take risks or move toward each other. Doors slam shut because no one bothers to tweak them open. For example, if and when we don't know what to "call" another person, all we have to do is ask. "Do you prefer to be called African-American or black?" Or, "May I use your first name?" Learning to ask questions is a very holy activity.

At the same time, many diversity specialists argue that the best way to handle religious differences is to be your own person and to speak on behalf of your own God. They point to the embarrassment of trying to relate by speaking "Southern" or "urban." "Hey, man, what's up?" a suburban person may say to someone from the inner city. If the suburban person usually speaks that way, then there is no big issue. But when a suburban person changes speech in order to "connect" with an urban person, there is often an embarrassment, a sense of being talked down to on the part of the other.

The holy use of the tongue in a multicultural environment makes a lot of people nervous. Instead, we can think of it as an enormous festival—where we ask lots of questions of each other as opposed to issuing lots of statements.

Speech That Carries Spirit

I was giving a speech to a fairly conservative group of Christians. The topic was my interfaith marriage. I knew there was disapproval lurking in the crowd—and I almost didn't want to give the speech.

Then I got an idea. I would talk about what I—allergic to fundamentalisms of just about any kind—like about religious fundamentalists.

I spoke of religious fundamentalists' passion, their urgency for the right answer to the question, their joy in the truth and the certain knowledge of salvation. I spoke of myself in a self-deprecating way; my uncertainty about most matters drives people of a more conservative bent crazy. I told them what they didn't like about me—that I was wishy-washy, capable of having dozens of answers to the same question. I got them laughing about what they hate about liberals and open-minded types. Then I made my point. God loves me and the people to whom I am allergic. I don't have to be right about God to be loved.

Sacred speech actively reaches to love its "enemy." Jesus even says we are to love our enemies, and the Dalai Lama says that our "enemy" is always our best teacher. There is a nonviolence to sacred speech that lies at its heart. Because nonviolence will win out, we find ourselves praising even the obstacles in the way to world peace.

Likewise, the strategy of asking questions can take us a long way toward public sacred speech. Asking questions implies praise: "I want to know more about you. I don't think I know everything. I think I can be improved by knowing more about you." Asking a question shows that we know we don't know something. Intercultural respect often begins in knowing what we don't know. Questions open doors.

Often, the start to publicly good language is the opening of the many doors that were previously shut. Praising a world where the doors seem closed and where "loss" is the primary word for experience is difficult. It is easy to praise a world where we think we can gain. Many people of color don't really want to hear what white people have to say: They feel they have heard enough. Likewise, many white people feel they have a lot to say but don't dare say it because they have lost their previous pinnacle. Learning to speak again—as recovering racists, which I, being white, often call myself—is challenging and worth every risk it involves. Sacred speech praises the real world; it does not retreat to a world that might have been or "should" have been.

Speech That Carries Spirit

At the train station in New Haven, Connecticut, I ask to buy a ticket to Bridgeport, a primarily black city about twenty minutes away. The ticket salesperson, who is also white, says to me, "You don't want to go there." "Why?" I ask, even though I know what he is saying. He senses my suspicion. "What, you think I'm a racist because I am trying to warn you about Bridgeport?" "No, I don't think you are a racist because you don't want me to go to Bridgeport. . . ." This is the time to pause, once a quarrel has equilibrium. This is the time to figure out what you really want out of the conversation. My "agenda" was at first to shame this man. He had angered and upset me. Shame, however, would not have resulted in any positive education. Instead, it would result in negative education; to this salesperson, I would be the kind of white person who is almost as bad as those people in Bridgeport. I paused. He paused. He gave me the ticket. Lightly, or as lightly as I could under the circumstances, I said, "I have a good friend in Bridgeport. She is very ill. I'm sorry I am so jumpy today."

I have moved from being the kind of strong, direct, judgmental person who can't teach the ticket clerk anything to being the kind of vulnerable human being he might be able to respect. The strategic use of weakness is important to sacred speech. It might even be considered strength. Yes, we have to be very careful not to manipulate either our strength or our weakness. But we need to keep from turning every conversation into a strength-to-strength battle. Weakness is a beautiful thing, especially if we can find a way to share it. Weakness can be as worthy of praise as strength.

It is crucial to establish a goal in any difficult conversation. I did want to educate the clerk at the train station. I did not want to shame him. I also wanted to visit my friend in Bridgeport. I enjoy a world with challenges and a world with diversity; that is the name of my praise. From there, I can take risks and sometimes even open doors. Praise is the font of sacred appreciation of the day and the way in which we live. To not praise the way things "are" is to be alienated from the sacred in both speech and life.

TO PRAISE GOD

Let me tell you a story about a long and winding road. It is the road to Machu Picchu, an ancient Incan settlement deep in the Andean mountains, at an altitude of 13,000 feet. To get there you must fly to Lima, then fly another hour to Custco, then take a train three hours to a town called Aqua Calientes. Then you get on a bus that miraculously manages to get you up to Machu Picchu. I say "miraculously" because the brakes don't sound that good, the guardrails on the side of the mountain are nonexistent, and the driver is blasé about the whole business. He has made the passage up and down the mountain so many times that he doesn't notice that he is making it.

What goes up must come down. The rocks of Machu Picchu get cold as the sun goes down—and it goes down early because the mountains around it are so high. We get back on the bus. As everywhere else in Peru, children are selling things outside the bus. "Please, *amiga*," they say, "buy this. This is different. This is quality. This is what you need to take home." Some of the children even call me Señorita, that's how eager they are to make a sale. Sounds like normal American life, doesn't it, where everywhere you look someone wants to sell you something? Buy this, buy that. Buy this item, this point of view, this theory, this lifestyle, this, that. Buy, buy, buy, amigos. But there at the side of this bus, the last one down the mountain for that day, stands a group of children in traditional Andean dress, making music with their pipes and posing for photo ops. They aren't selling anything—and therefore our eyes are drawn to them. There is something godly about the children: They are a step beyond the world of the exchange, on the edge of an ancient temple. Then the chill of evening sets in, and the bus heads down the long and winding road.

At the first hairpin curve, a girl from the group of traditionally dressed children appears out of nowhere, singing, saying good-bye. The bus passengers laugh and wave. Then the bus makes another circle. The girl appears again and sings and waves. Another circle, another girl. And on down the entire mountain, this child races the bus through the hills and meets it at every curve. There is a sense of pure joy in the child as she energetically

To praise the world
To praise God
To praise our own life
These are our objectives. Praise is the sacred speech of the spiritual detective. No matter what happens, we look for the God and the good in it. No matter what.

greets the bus. We imagine her knowing these ancient trails. We imagine her as what a child should be, having fun, playfully racing a bus down a hill. Not selling souvenirs at the side of the road. For the twenty-minute ride, the child gives us all the equivalent of a nightclub show. Song, dance, action, movement.

Then comes the cover charge. At the bottom of the hill, the girl is let onto the bus by the driver and opens her purse. She wants a tip. You can hear the groan. Some people say that she isn't a girl at all but a boy because of the strength it takes to race the bus down the mountain.

My point is about a winding, curvy road. My point is that God mixes in with commerce and is not "pure" or unalloyed. On the edge of great temples we can find God—if we are looking. God doesn't have to be praised only in a church or a synagogue or a mosque.

Sacred speech can happen on a tourist bus. "That is no girl, that's a boy," my seat companion says. "Who cares?" I say. "I care," she says. "I feel used. I feel set up. I got dragged into the freedom of his running down the hill. I thought finally someone was going to give me something for free. I wanted to believe in an older Peru, a less needy one. It breaks my heart to see these children beg." "Do you still think God is in those rocks at Machu Picchu?" I have to ask. "Yes, of course." "Well, then, God is in that boy or girl too. She or he has to eat." The very cleverness of the child's effort gets my praise! And I do see God in it. We have to be able to have strong words—not weak words—in sacred speech.

Was that girl working or playing with the bus? At which layer do we want to move into life? The upper layer, where all is beautiful and free and simple, until the sun sets and the rocks get cold? The middle layer, where we find ourselves careening down a hill with no guardrails, only entertainment to keep us sane? The bottom layer, where we realize there is a price to life, that sometimes seven-year-old girls have to work buses to stay alive?

I like to call such layering of sacred speech and interpretation "the action of grace within us." Sacred speech carries us to God in informal ways, such as the act of interpretation of an experience. Where is God in the experience? How do we move from lament to praise? What might God be saying to us? Where is the grace in the situation? Grace means that we are safe, that disappointment can't really hurt us. Grace also means that even hungry girls are safe. And it means that we are free, that no one can own us, that we are happy. There is no sadness that can compete with our joy. Sacred speech is not a "technique" for talking holy; it is instead an expression of what we know about Spirit. Sacred speech comes from living intimately with God.

Such living also means that we can blunder. No mistake we make is sufficiently large to remove us from God's love. We are free to take risks and make mistakes. Lewis Thomas in *The Medusa and the Snail* says that "the capacity to blunder slightly is the real marvel of DNA. Without this special attribute, we would still be anaerobic bacteria and there would be no music. . . . Biology needs a better word than error for the driving force in evolution. Or maybe error will do after all, when you remember that it came from an old root meaning to wander about, looking for something."[2] I love that last line. To wander about looking for something is the meaning of error and the meaning of blundering forward.

Many of us find the enormity of the power of the Holy in our lives is more than we can manage. We are almost afraid of its rock-hard truth, its sizable security, and its enormous power to ground our lives and give us the capacity to stand against captivity of any kind. Thus, we fiddle. We fuss about human reality on our way down the hill from Machu Picchu. We let details get in our way. We think like children about God when long ago we became too old for that. Or we become literal. We become scared of the fundamentalists, who sometimes seem to have all but destroyed the sacred by hitting people over the head with it.

I daresay that child in Machu Picchu is blundering and running down the hill this very afternoon looking for a tip at the end of his or her road. Is she unholy because she asks for a tip? I think not.

One of my favorite Christian Scriptures is John 15:11. "I have said these things to you so that my joy may be in you, and that your joy may be complete." I have always been fascinated by what it might mean to find joy complete in us. Would all the laundry have to be folded and world peace achieved? Or might there be joy and praise in the middle time, in the middle of our journey on muddling roads? I think the latter. Sacred speech expresses what we know of the middle road and the middle joy. It teaches us to see what is already there.

SACRED SPEECH
IN WORSHIP

We can locate God's activity anywhere, at any time, and praise it. But we can also formally dedicate time to prayer. Liturgical words are surely sacred and surely beautiful; they serve to praise.

Worship services are rehearsals of the good time God has promised as destiny for the world. They are a time to remember the ancient texts and to think about them in a contemporary context. They are a time to sing. They are a time to forget about ourselves. A time to be quiet together. A time for filtered light. A time for lit candles. A time for preludes and postludes, marked beginnings and endings. Worship is a time to let go of the past, to receive a blessing, to be told that it is possible to go on. It is a time to learn more about the core of the universe, a time to end the week, and a time to prepare for the week. It is a time to be in sanctuary, safe space, to look out the windows and know we are secure inside.

Worship is time out of time. It is time that ends one week and begins another. Worship keeps time by keeping the beat. It gets us out of one kind of time into another kind of time on behalf of the very time we left. Without worship, the weeks get strange. In worship, we learn to press our stop key and our start key.

I have learned to be less "churchy" about worship. I have learned that God is not caged in a building and that worship is not, either. Most certainly, God is not the end point of my liturgical efforts! We can find God in almost any regular practice. We can even find God in irregular practice. God is not present only at our bidding: God is also present in our lives unbidden.

Having said that formal worship is not everything, I then need to say that formal worship is something. The liturgical language of our faiths is indeed sacred. It is beautiful. It is well worn. It is worth knowing, even knowing by heart.

This bidding hymn is a great one to memorize.

Come, my Way, my Truth, my Life: such a way as gives us breath; such a truth as ends all strife; such a life as conquers death.

Come my Light, my Feast, my Strength: such a light as shows a feast; such a feast as mends in length; such a strength as makes a guest.

Come my Joy, my Love, my Heart: such a joy as none can move; such a love as none can part; such a heart as joys in love.[3]

Another entire book could be written about how liturgical language is a sacred language. Let this one beautiful hymn stand as a small example of a large treasury.

TO PRAISE OUR OWN LIFE

Praise is surely one way of looking at the world. It is detective work for God in normal human experiences as well as in formal liturgical worship. Praise is also an attitude toward our own days. Sacred speech often tells stories from our lives in such a way that we detect the godliness in the details. In fact, learning to observe details in a daily way is a sure form of opening our mouths for praise. We speak what we see and that beautifies it.

If, when I woke up this morning, all I knew was that I started the coffeemaker, woke up my daughter with her favorite nickname, brought her a cappuccino and helped her rage at a friend who was behaving inconsiderately, kissed my husband, let the dog out, fed the cat, et cetera, I would be missing so much of what was actually happening. It is fourteen days until my daughter's seventeenth birthday. These are the last days of "sweet sixteen" she is ever going to have. It is her last month of her junior year of high school. These grades matter more than most do. Yes, the cat was nervous again this morning and played the in-and-out game. The other cat died ten days ago—did I enjoy his idiosyncrasies enough? Now I miss him terribly. I can be aware of the life I am living while I am living it—or I can suspend myself above it and know only gratitude in grief or loss. Sacred speech lets us know gratitude in the moment. Thank God I have a daughter and a cat!

I learned way too much about the preciousness of daily time when I had breast cancer. I was bombarded with clichés—that I was at war with cancer, that I had to win the fight, that if anyone could win the fight I could, and on and on, in a militarizing of the experience that offended me. I knew the sacred speech of daily praise; I knew how to see what I was living when I was living it. The better therapy for me was to stay grateful for the good of what is and was—and not wage war for more life. I needed to learn how to see even more deeply the hours and minutes I had.

I remember taking the Christmas tree down for what might have been the last time. Instead of rushing the ornaments to their boxed beds, I caressed them. I didn't want to say good-bye so much as hello! I wanted to let these little mementos know that I knew them and that they had made me glad. When they come back next year, I will see them differently. I will notice them. There were many years when I did not. I'd rather fight indifference than cancer any day.

I also remember one man in my parish being terrifically upset with me at that time. He thought my use of inclusive language in worship was "ruining" his church. (We sing "Creator, Christ, and Holy Ghost" instead of "Father, Son, and Holy Ghost" for the doxology, on the grounds that "Father" is only one name for God.) He delivered a letter to the congregation asking for my resignation during one of our Friday night "wine and cheese" monthly events. I had enjoyed enough wine to be happy. I was trying on a strawberry costume, which we were going to use to make a funny announcement for the annual strawberry fair organized by this man's wife. When he arrived, I greeted him dressed as a strawberry. He handed me the letter asking for my resignation. I was laughing at the thought that we were talking as one strawberry to another and that it is the rare pastor who has to greet angry parishioners wearing a large strawberry. I had breakfast with him the next morning and listened ardently to his concerns. But for that one moment in a long drama of dissension and conversation, I had a sacred experience. He couldn't have picked a better time to show up. From then on I did not "war" with him. I just remembered the strawberry and God's incredible sense of humor.

Other details of life bring me a joy that cancer can't steal. My eldest son was on his way to his first day of college. Sure enough, he nicked his lip while shaving—and arrived at school looking utterly ridiculous. To him it was a major crisis; for me, it was a way of sending him off, wounded, like the wound that existed in me as I let him go.

Likewise, the first time I touched the wound on my body where my breast had been, I found myself outside of cancer-cliché land. I had asked around and discovered that many women were as chicken as I was about touching the wound. I had to create a little ceremony just to get myself ready for the ache. And I did. Very often sacred speech needs the lift of liturgy to get itself going.

Living a life of clichés is not living a life of praise. Finding our way beyond clichés is living a life of praise. We find ourselves saying quite often, "How could I have made that up?" That's the life of praise: It is original, not copied. It knows itself. And it is deeply glad to be alive, even in normal, quotidian time.

4

To Pray

Prayer leads us to a sacred space widely understood as liminal, or threshold, space. Liminal space is a concept discussed by Victor Turner in his books on ritual, celebration, and performance. By liminal he means edgy, between Heaven and earth, alive with more than is normally perceived. Prayer is an ancient form of sacred speech that takes us to God through words; prayer takes us to the liminal, to our tiptoes. There we stand and squint and look deeply into the cosmos. God meets us there on our verbal tiptoes.

Prayer is practicing being in the presence of God, usually using words, though gestures can suffice. By gestures, I mean yoga or tai chi, kneeling or arm waving, folding hands and bowing the head, davening, or any of a thousand poses that place us in the presence of God. Sacred speech is often prayerful, addressing God directly by name or by breath.

For some people, intimacy with Spirit is simple; for others, it is very difficult. Spirit is not affected by whether we can speak or not. Instead, we are met by God as we make the approach.

Oddly, many of us think of ourselves in the driver's seat when it comes to God. We think that it is our job to find God, believe in God, create God, give birth to God, tend God, worship God, and take God to the grocery store. It is not. God is our parent. God is like our father. God is like our mother. God seeks us out much more than we could ever seek God out. When people tell me they don't believe in God, I always want to say in return, "But which God don't you believe in?" Many of us don't believe in the God we set up as our creation, our son or daughter, our manifestation of a foxhole, that last-ditch hiding place of soldiers in war. Why should we? But not to believe in the God who seeks us out is another matter entirely.

Speech That Carries Spirit

A man in my parish had been talking to me for a long time about how he just couldn't believe in God. Then his son was in a terrible car accident. The son was being transported by helicopter to Massachusetts General Hospital. The father said to me as we lifted off, "Donna, the God I don't believe in is right here right now...." God shows up. God seeks us out. God is like that. God has never stopped looking for a lost child in any grocery store in the world. God shows up when people are in trouble, whether bidden by words or not.

Many self-reliant people find themselves in situations where they need help. Many adults need a parent; we may be parents but we

still need the protection of a parent ourselves. Prayer is a reach for
protection from a "heavenly" parent. Many mothers feel widowed,
even if they have a husband. Many fathers feel orphaned, even if they
have a mother and a father. Many mothers feel very alone—as though
no one cared about them and their only job was to care for others. If
you want to make a mother cry, put on Ella Fitzgerald singing,
"Sometimes I feel like a motherless child." Get ready for that verse
from "Someone to Watch over Me."

God knows. God is protector, not protected. God is watching,
not watched for. God is our parent and we are protected. God resides
in holy habitation. In prayer, we move to the place where God lives.
God is at home for us. We move through the borders of earth toward
Heaven when we pray. The sacred words of prayer don't "make"
God appear; they take us to the God who is already there.

Much has been made of the "inner child" by psychologists. I
believe there is also an inner orphan in many people, the part our parents failed to touch or couldn't touch. And I believe there is an inner
widow in each of us, the part our partner failed to touch or couldn't
touch. God touches these parts when others fail us: That is the point
of prayer. The old hymn says, "We should never be discouraged, take
it to the Lord in prayer."

For the sacred speech of prayer to happen, we cannot become so
wrapped up in the horizontal dimensions of our lives that we ignore
the vertical. We get so wrapped up in our daily lives and "to do's"
that we forget simply to be. We lose our way and forget that we are
protected. We think we are all earth and not also a bit of Heaven, all
chronos and not also a bit of eternity. We forget where we are unless
we reach for God in prayer. Again, prayer is practicing the preexist-
ing presence of God. We can do so by breathing, by speaking, by

sighing, by raising our fist, by opening our hands. Sometimes a gesture that is personal and customized is better than a lot of words. We go to the liminal by the words and the gesture combined—as when we fold our hands or drop to our knees. Then we find that God has found us.

Likewise, some of the most beautiful words in the world are the words put in prayers. I think of the Twenty-third Psalm, which many religious people have committed to memory. I use this psalm whenever I am truly scared, such as before surgery or at the bedside of someone who is suffering terribly.

Once, when I was in training at a mental hospital, I recited the psalm to a very sick woman who was all alone. I broke up in the recitation—and she completed it through my tears for both of us. I'll never forget that she remembered, "Yea though I walk through the valley of the shadow of death, I will fear no evil, for Thou art with me, Thy rod and thy staff they comfort me, Thou anoints my head with oil, My cup runs over. . . ." I'll never forget the words as said by a seventy-six-year-old mentally ill person in her last five minutes. She died when she completed the psalm, "Surely goodness and mercy shall follow me all the days of my life and I shall dwell in the house of the Lord forever." She let the prayer of the psalm take her to liminal space, from which space she died.

PERSONAL PRAYER

Many people customize their own prayer life by listing their loved ones as they go to sleep or as they wake. Others give thanks for at least one thing every day and confess one thing every night as they reach for sleep. Still others recite the Lord's Prayer upon waking or at noon. Muslims bow to Mecca five times a day, in a discipline that clearly keeps God at the top of their minds, as opposed to hidden in some faraway psychological space, only to be hauled out in the event of a life interruption by a foxhole or a car accident. Still other people thank God only over food and

> Prayer is the practice of being in the presence of God. It is a reach toward God that can be done bodily, with speech, with thought, and with sighs too deep for words. We have to learn how to pray; practice makes perfect.

drink. Others pray weekly on the Sabbath with the lighting of candles. In my view, it does not matter to God how we pray; it does matter that we pray, that we reach, that we practice being in the presence of God. God will come to us even if we do not pray. But once we know how to pray, we are able to enjoy the presence of God more regularly and more deeply.

God wants maturity for us. Maturity is the capacity to receive horizontal love but not to depend on it. Sacred speech is a vehicle of maturity. It teaches us love and frees us from fear. Theologians join psychologists in speaking negatively of both dependency and independence—and hope for some kind of interdependence between spouses or between mature parents and their children. I like an additional criterion, something people call transdependence, or reliance on God. God is the dependable one—the rest of us, as givers and takers, are less so. Mature mothers rely on God, not on their spouses. Mature parents rely on God, not on their grown children. Grown children rely on God, not on their parents for affirmation.

God loves us better than we love each other. That is my point. We try to love each other as unconditionally and as well as God loves us—but usually we fail. Prayer carries us to the unconditional love of God. We can express it in our speech.

I think back to one of the bad moments in my own marriage, one that repeats itself every now and then. It has to do with pride and conceit, two characteristics completely absent from the mind and heart of God. When one of our children had a certain problem, I said we should apply solution 74 to the problem (let's call it that for the sake of the story). My husband, Warren, insisted on seeing a specialist and spent an enormous amount of money on it. He returned from the doctor's office elated and announced that we should apply solution 74 to the problem. I was steamed. I was livid. How could he accept a doctor's wisdom instead of mine, since it was the same wisdom? Unlike God, I want approvals that I don't get. God never asks us to approve God's behavior. God simply behaves. God never asks us to grovel before God's wisdom. Instead, God just keeps protecting and watching and caring and showing up.

Since that original episode with the doctor, there have been many others. I think I have said something, no one hears me, and then they repeat back from some other source what I said. I call these repeats "Cox-Steiners" (the name of the doctor consulted that first time). No, I am not modest about my immodesty.

Think again of God. God must hear Cox-Steiners all day long. But God doesn't go ballistic or get steamed. God encourages us to be wise ourselves.

On a personal level, prayer brings us to the throne of grace, the sight of God, even if all we do is point toward the vertical dimension of life as we know it. God doesn't really care whether we pray well or frequently or "right"; instead, God cares for us. That is the whole point. Mature people enjoy the presence of God; from it, we can derive grace.

PUBLIC PRAYER
CAN BE CHALLENGING

Prayer in public immediately gets us into the question of whose God is being addressed. Is it "our" God or "their" God? Do we speak against God when we pray to too small a God? I think so.

I pray a lot in public and use this prayer intentionally as a way to name God openly and inclusively.

> Almighty God, Thou beyond any name or captivity by words or flesh, Thou whom some call Yahweh, and others call Adonai, and others speak of only as breath; Thou whom some call Allah, whom I know as Jesus and as Christ, Thou whom some call Spirit and others call Higher Power and others call Force and others know as inner fire, draw near. Let what we do here be holy, even as you are holy and beyond any name. Amen.

Still, many people who also pray in public conclude their prayer, "In Jesus' name," if they happen to be Christian. Such prayer can be very offensive to Jews, people of other faiths, and nonbelievers. Sacred speech prays. Sacred speech practices the presence of God. Sacred speech is polite; it is not exclusive, just as God is not exclusive. Does that mean that Christians should not pray to Jesus when they pray with other Christians? Of course not! Instead, we should understand that Jesus is one of many wonderful ways to God. When we pray with our family, alone, or in our own parochial community, we may pray to the God whose particular name we have been taught. When we pray in public, we may pray to the God who is beyond any name we have been taught.

There are many people who think that interfaith or multifaith prayer is impossible. I do not. In fact, I think the very risks we take in praying openly are a holy risk, an intentional placing of ourselves in liminal space.

A personal pattern of prayer that is inclusive can be employed in the family by leaving out denominational names for God and using more inclusive words. In our family, as a table grace, we have created a gesture prayer, precisely so that people of many faiths will be comfortable at our table.

> God be above us, God be below us, God be all around us, and God be with our friends . . . and those we want as friends. Amen.

As we say this prayer, we raise our hands, lower our hands, make a circle with our hands, and then join hands. The very use of hands is a bodily way to pray beyond words that often captures and delimits. I just taught this prayer to a four-year-old girl, who taught it to her dolls. Her favorite doll's name is Plato—and she adds Plato's name at the end of her prayer.

Prayer is in certain ways the most sacred of speech: It is what happens between us and God. That doesn't mean that what happens between human beings is not godly; instead, it is less direct, more muted, more slanted. God is present in our interactions with each other; in prayer, we address God directly.

Practicing how to be in the presence of God in a multifaith and interfaith context is crucial. A group of clergy had all gathered for a prayer service: Four rabbis, two priests, five ministers . . . all wanting to pray their own way. As they planned the service, they got into quite an argument over the content of the bulletin for the service. Should it be an interfaith service, implying that we are all unified in what we say? Or should it be a multifaith service, implying that our diversities are all safely present? No one answered the question. The bulletin ended up with the simple title "Prayers for Peace."

The day will come when we will pray in public together and do it well. That day will come as many languages are spoken and heard more regularly—as Babel becomes more basic—and we learn to trust the liminal space of God. We are in Diversity 101 class in this new century. We can count on growing and maturing in words and actions, especially if we can simply pray—that is, practice being in the presence of God in public and enter the liminal space where God lives.

PRAYERS TO THE
CLOSER FACE OF GOD

Many traditions have prayers to the "transcendent" face of God. These prayers go to the God of eternity, cosmos, Heaven, far "above" humanity. There are also ways to pray to the "immanent," or closer, face of God. I created the prayers below as a way for people to open themselves to sacred speech when they pray together in public. You may want to use them at gatherings or write your own prayers for a particular event.

Ordinary Prayer
Ancient of Days, Eternal God, beginning and end, you who keep all things and all people together, be with us in our part of eternity today. Strengthen our best intentions and let the rest go by, that we may know the importance of this day in your grander scheme. Arouse a sense of vocation in us, that our name has been called, and use us. In the name of all those humans who found their way to Spirit. Amen.

For Those Who Work for Peace and Justice
Let us pray for those who work for peace and justice.

Let the peoples tremble, O God, let all the peoples tremble, at the evil which threatens Thy earth, our life, our breath, and our hope.

Let the peoples praise Thee, O God, let all the peoples praise Thee by stopping bombs, by rejoicing in life, by making fragile hope sturdy and steadfast.

Turn fear and trembling, O God, to praise and action, and grant us Thy Peace. Amen.

For the Safety of Children
If the world were a wider place, O God, I would make my children's way gentle. Sometimes they will have to go through a narrow and mean place. Help them, O God.

When There Is Conflict
Send down a deep root, when there is conflict. Drive us to the core of reality, which is our love for each other. Let us learn to live from there, and not from hurt. Keep partners together. Don't let the kids get between them. And if they do, come and stand in the middle, O God, and hold them up. In the name of the Spirit who knew the middle places, the stuck places, the meaning of triangle. Amen.

Prayers for Teenagers
I

When my parents fight, it scares me so much. Help me get help, God. Show me the right person to talk to. Amen.

II

Strange things are happening in my body. I don't feel like me anymore. I get madder than I ever have. Tears come out of nowhere. I feel like I could hurt someone if I'm not careful—

and sometimes I do. I made my mother cry and don't even know why. Steady me, O God. Amen.

III
Spirit, make people stop asking me what I'm going to do when I grow up. Let me just be here, now. Amen.

IV
When people say I look just like my father, or mother, I cringe. Don't they know how different I am? You know, right God, you know. Amen.

5

To Judge

In forgiveness and praise and prayer, we are often on the happy side of the emotional scale. We are restored in forgiveness; we are glad in praise; we are linked to Spirit in prayer. But sacred speech travels the entire emotional spectrum, not just the happy side. Sacred speech can be employed to tell difficult truths. "To tell the truth in love" was one of my ordination vows. It has been the hardest to keep. Sometimes the truth gets disconnected from the love—and sometimes the love gets disconnected from the truth. We can find ourselves unwilling to judge, as many partners who stay with alcoholics too long can tell you. Or we find ourselves all too willing to judge—and condemn all who try to get close to us.

Speech That Carries Spirit

The chair of an important committee was opposing everything that I or any other member of the parish brought to his attention. He even blocked accessibility repairs to the church—with a man in a wheelchair willing to donate the money to make such repairs. I spent hours talking to this chairman, trying to figure out what he was blocking. The mission of his committee was to facilitate the program of the church through the building—but he wouldn't allow a decision to be made. Other members were complaining, not just the befuddled man in the wheelchair.

I finally had to ask the chairman to resign. I had to wait until I could do it without blasting him with my anger. He had wasted so many hours of my time—I was furious at myself and at him for letting this waste happen. But I couldn't avoid the hurt that I had tossed in his lap. The truth in love was the destination; I am not sure I got all the way there. But I at least saw the map in my hand. And he and I have found ways to be friends.

Sacred speech does not rule out anger. Instead, it tames and uses it. Anger can be a very positive prelude to justice and judgment. Surely anger was a vital tool for women in America in the 1970s. It enabled new perspectives, new understandings of oppressive conditions that had previously been unmentioned. Anger had a strong link to raising consciousness: It let things come out that otherwise were buried. "I couldn't believe—still can't—how angry I could become, from deep down and way back, something like a 5,000-year buried anger," Robin Morgan declared in *Sisterhood Is Powerful.* "Every black woman in America lives her life somewhere along a wide curve of ancient and unexpressed angers," Audre Lorde once observed.

And yet so many of us so much want not to be angry! We can't deny how angry we can get—either at ancient injustice or at another driver on the highway. We want to be beyond that. Anger hurts us as well as the targets of our rage.

One does not have to be a feminist to understand this kind of rage. We see it on the highway all the time. Sacred speech is prepared for the rage of rage. Sacred speech has a gesture for the highway when someone tries to hurt us or take over our lane. I often suggest to those who are prone to road rage that they use a nonaggressive hand gesture, something like Tevye used during his famous laments in *Fiddler on the Roof*. Instead of judgment against road assailants, we can lift our fist to the sky in a lament to the gods. (After all, traffic is as much their fault as it is ours, right?) A good one-handed gesture—aimed not at the other driver—allows us to give back to the cosmos what has just been given to us. Judging the other driver is probably stupid, and it unnecessarily raises our blood pressure.

Anger grows from a messy buildup, as the Berenstain Bears would say, because nothing was done at the time of small violations. When we rage at our Internet provider or our fellow drivers, we are also raging at ourselves for living in a world where we "must" drive and where we "must" access the Web. We know that driving is as morally difficult as other institutionalized difficulties. We know that road rage is an exquisitely modern difficulty, one in which we are complicit, and one in which others may have as much of a gripe against us as we do against them.

When we don't say anything about the small steps on our toes, we fly into a rage over someone knocking us down. When we don't notice that some of our trouble comes from our own behavior, such as driving way beyond the loss of the ozone layer, we are inclined to the insanity of judgment. Judgment can be insane (that is, not making any rational sense) and it can be sane, making rational sense. The distinction is to judge appropriately, with anger suitable to the actual matter at hand. Road rage often goes off the deep end. Rage at sexism also goes off the deep end. At the same time, there are some drivers who need to be reported immediately to the police. And there are some men who sneak "feels" of women on subway cars. Judgment manages difficult matters as they arise. It does not collect them. From a manageable matter, we often move to unmanageable matters by our earlier silence. Judgment is sacred speech when it manages matters as they arise.

SACRED SPEECH
IS NOT SILENT

This chapter approaches the concept of sacred speech in previous chapters from another angle, asking the question, "Why didn't anybody say anything?" It's a question we unfortunately hear much too often. This chapter helps us take the risks involved in "saying something." It gives us examples that take us over and through the risks involved in nonviolent or loving behavior and underlines the connection of risk-taking love to virtue in holy speech. Often "nobody said anything" because nobody was secure enough to take a risk. They—and we—thought that fear should prevail. Of course, when fear prevails, trouble multiplies. There are alternatives—and one of them is learning to speak the truth in love. Holy speech teaches itself how to speak the truth in love. Although the truth is not only judgment, it can be judgment. Judgment is not the opposite of love or forgiveness or even praise so much as it is one of the stops on the road.

Sometimes holy speech has to get to the "bottom" of the trouble, like a plumber's snake unclogs deep, long-buried blocks. Psychotherapy is that kind of holy speech. Rarely, though, do non-professional counselors need the plumber's snake. Instead, we need the ability to go on, to move forward, and to stop repeating the accusations and claims of the past.

Speech That Carries Spirit

The writer had let her editor at the newspaper make the same mistake in spelling about three times. The editor said she was wrong in spelling the word her way, but she knew she was right. It wasn't a big deal, just the question of whether an additional vowel should be used. One version of the spelling was British English, the other American English. *Behavior* and *behaviour* are just two different versions of the same word; depending on where the work was published, either could be correct. She was sure that both spellings were acceptable, but she was too afraid to prove it because her editor was a fairly sensitive person. She had seen others correct her, even when they were right, and things had deteriorated.

She wished she had done the poetic version of "You say tomato and I say tomato, you say potato and I say potato" the first time it had occurred. That way she wouldn't have been so mad when she finally wrote her humorous poem. The sarcasm and anger that seeped into the poem sank it. Earlier, and more lightly, she might have had a chance at genuine humor and exchange. She "had" to include the thrice-occurring nature of the error. As a result, she blew it. Instead of a good laugh, the editor got predictably sensitive and became even more nit-picky in her review of the writer's work. She lost what she might have won.

Judgment can be done lightly or heavily, repentantly or retribu-
tively. We can often win by losing a little. We can often gain relationship by refusing to "win" arguments.

In sacred speech, we are less the plumber getting to the root of
the blockage than we are the gardener planting the small tree today
that will cast shade eighty years from now. A proverb helps: "When
should we have planted the tree to give us shade today? Eighty years
ago." Now is the time for sacred speech, no matter how small or
insignificant it seems to be.

Many of us think that judgment will lead to trouble. We fear
that "if we say something," there will be retribution. We will find
ourselves in more trouble. We let fear rule us and end up in the very
trouble we were trying to avoid. We "internalize" the oppression we
fear may come from the outside. One great argument for learning
how to judge in sacred ways, ways connected to love, is that of
repression. When we repress our anger, we oppress ourselves. We
don't need an outside enemy anymore.

Dr. Seuss understood this matter. He published *The 500 Hats of
Bartholomew Cubbins* in 1938. He surely didn't intend for
Bartholomew to be a secret agent for the holy but, like many things
in the story, something like that simply happened. Bartholomew can't
help disobeying the king's order that he respectfully remove his hat—
because a new hat keeps appearing as soon as he takes off the offend-
ing one—and that makes all the difference in his life. The truth has a
way of coming out, even in front of the king. The Bartholomew para-
ble teaches a lot about sacred speech. We will say what we have to
say *anyway,* so why not speak the truth first?

We also wear "unconscious" hats, and they keep coming out, no
matter what we do to repress them. We too arrive before "kings" more

often than we realize. Some of these would-be kings are offices and some are unnecessarily boring classrooms and some are highways too crowded to welcome us or our humanity. Such things rule us, especially if we give them permission to do so. Some of them are coworkers who are not doing their jobs. Some chair our key committees. We arrive needing words that have ointments and prayer books attached to them. Phony gods of all kinds are begging us to tip our hats to them. Far too often, too many of us do tip our hats to the phony kings and the phony gods. Learning the art of sacred speech, the soft refusal, the sturdy judgment, and the capacity to believe our own discernment of what is true and false for us—these keep us from bowing down at the wrong time. They keep us from the dangerous repression of doing what false authorities want us to do. We learn to say no on behalf of a larger yes.

Judgment can be a sacred act. It can say no at the right time on behalf of loving affirmation of larger principles.

Speech That Carries Spirit

Julia Fournier is a repentant gambler who goes to the Port Authority every day to sit near the Atlantic City gates. She spoke to the *New York Times* about her hopes for a reunion with her daughter, who she says abandoned her there a year ago. Her daughter said, "Choose gambling or choose me." Julia chose gambling.

Someone said they saw her daughter, cruising in circles around the Port Authority. Julia responded, "No, she wasn't looking for me . . . not after a year. But sometimes when I am at the Port Authority now, I think that maybe if I go and look on another street and stand there and wait a little, maybe I'll see her cruising around. Then I'd call out to her. And if she sees me, maybe she'll hug me tender and take me in her car. I hope. I'd cry and tell her I don't go to Atlantic City anymore."

When we fail to judge, we can cause a great deal of harm. Silence in the face of trouble, whether racism or sexism or homophobia or thoughtlessness, hurts people. In 1963, Martin Luther King Jr. said, "We will have to repent in this generation not merely for the hateful words and actions of the bad people but for the appalling silence of the good people." Audre Lorde often says the same thing only more acutely: "Your silence will not protect you."

I remember hearing about a rabbi who came to South Beach in Miami to a new congregation. At first he was widely acclaimed as "open-minded" with regard to the predominantly gay community. But then his failure to use the term "partners" instead of "husbands and wives" in his first sermon excited a storm. He lost his first gay members. Why? His language was exclusive.

Sacred speech is careful. Sacred speech receives judgment with grace. When excluded people, such as the gay community, raise issues about language, we often say they are being "politically correct." We might also say thank you. We might also know how God would respond. God doesn't respond with a loud, crashing, "I'm *always right.*" God receives our pain that something hurtful has happened.

But at the same time, when we know how to use sacred speech, we don't just walk out on the rabbi who makes one mistake. We make our judgment with a back door attached to it. We judge face to face, speaking our pain. And we have hope in the ability of the other to change. Instead of running away in flight or attacking in fight, we judge with grace. We judge with a door open to our future relationship.

A flyer distributed to members of a temple charges fifty dollars per couple for the dinner offered as part of a temple program. A single woman calls in irate. Why? She has been excluded. The same principles apply here. The single woman can call in "irate" and probably just cause the office staff to be defensive. Or she can call in calmly, surely, assertively, and ask that in the future dinners be described as open to all members of the temple. Sacred speech does not fight or flee; it gets closer to people while retaining the capacity to judge. One of the clear ways we can tell when we are outside of sacred speech is that the other has become defensive and hurt. Although we can't take responsibility for all that occurs between people when judgment has to happen, we can work to reduce defensiveness. It doesn't help anything.

> When we judge, we say no on behalf of a larger yes.
>
> We exclude on behalf of a larger inclusion.
>
> We say what we don't like in order to clarify what we do like.
>
> Judgment can be a sacred act when done to maximize love, minimize fear, and link people and communities together.

An invitation to the local church welcomes "families." Many object: Their families are broken or nonexistent. Again, unintentionally, language excludes. The word *family* is often unintentionally used in an exclusive sense. It is important in this day and age to say "families of all kinds" in our formal announcements. Otherwise, we are acting outside the framework of love. Sacred speech is an act of love and an act that reduces fear. When we invite "families of all kinds," we do a lot to reduce fear in those who are often rejected. We love them in a little way. Making a judgment about exclusive language in a church bulletin is an act of love as well as one of judgment.

How do we find open words to substitute for closed words, inclusive ones for exclusive ones? How do we find language that is not so careful that we can't even speak and yet carries our meaning when we do open our mouths? Some would argue that *everyone* has become too sensitive. That we don't need to speak "politically correct" language or find a new way to sing hymns that start with "Rise up, O men of God." Others know what it means to trigger language rage, to be just downright mean in response to language that makes us feel bad, as "please rise" may do to a disabled person, or "men of God" does to some women. Language can hurt or heal. It can include or exclude. It can sound funny in its attempts to include. I heard in a recent speech, "What a piece of work is person." There is no humor, however, in being excluded. Those who have been put outside a circle, even simply in a conversation, know what I mean.

Even if we believe "everybody" has become too sensitive, there are few ways forward besides accepting the judgments of the overly sensitive. Why would we not accept these judgments? What do we get out of judging the judgments that offend us? Decoding messages and finding cues in a globalizing world is not easy. We are only limping toward it. I think of how many rabbis have told me how much it hurts to be at a public gathering and hear the prayer conclude with "in Jesus' name. Amen." Or how many African Americans have spoken of the insult of white people trying to talk "black" to them. Or the inappropriate use of Spanish, for instance, when we speak to bilingual persons as though they were monolingual. Often, in these cases, we use an impoverished and untutored Spanish, which compares poorly to the excellent English in our conversational partner.

Ethical behavior is finding words that heal and avoiding words that hurt. We may make fools of ourselves from time to time, but that is a much less serious problem than the one of excluding or hurting people. We don't need to be rudely judgmental about the language we use, such as interrupting a program because someone failed to say, "Will all who are able please rise?" as opposed to "Please stand." We don't need to be on a high moral quest or be self-righteous fools in our ethical judgments. Tone is crucial when we judge another, especially in public.

Instead, we can witness. Action always speaks louder than words. We can speak a language that includes and avoid a language that excludes. That witness will go a long way toward the large circle and large tent that we hope human community can be. We can become cultural brokers and cultural allies.

We can have good manners at ecumenical events and interfaith weddings and funerals. We can pray to the God beyond God and not insist on our own version. We can offer our criticism of someone else's public gaffe with good humor and grace and a welcoming smile on our face. Often our judgment can be helped by a self-deprecating sense of humor.

Although many of us will fall off our nonviolent bicycles and end up criticizing another person's language in a rude way, it is not the best we can do. We can speak the language we want to speak and forget about controlling other people's words. Again, witness achieves what criticism usually doesn't.

One caveat: There is a blessing in the anger of those who feel excluded, of the ones who pick up the phone and object to "couples" printed on the flyer, of those who ruin our event by claiming the floor and saying we are sexist, racist, homophobic, and the rest. As we witness, we can also give thanks for the blessing of the anger. What people are really saying is that they want "in," not to be left "out." That "wanting in" is a blessing; it translates as, "I want to be a part of you, not *not* a part of you."

We have known for a long time that ethnic jokes are only funny to some of us. We have known that they exclude and sometimes hurt. The foundation of society is people who really want "in." Why not open the doors?

Even and especially when we find ourselves using sacred words of judgment, we are asking to be let in. We are claiming the circle of good and positive humanity for ourselves. We are disclaiming the narrow versions of humanity on behalf of the larger and more open ones.

One of my church members who runs a very successful business says that every complaint she receives is a plea from the customer to get closer to her and her wares. She welcomes complaints! When we welcome judgments and those who judge, we do the same. We widen the circle of our friends and decrease the circle of our enemies. Thus, love and freedom from fear are marks of judgment. These marks make it holy.

It is important to remember that no one likes to be judged. Most people are extraordinarily sensitive to judgment. We remember the one negative remark after a sermon even if a hundred positive ones have been stated. We remember the teacher's comment on our paper that was critical and forget the praise. We do not have thick skins. I have long recommended that my fellow clergy wear "bulletproof vestments" so that we don't get as wounded as we do when people criticize our gifts and offerings. When we are trying to reduce fear and enhance love in sacred speaking, we have to be very careful in our judgments. We will inevitably hurt the person who is listening to us. We have to know that, feel it, be conscious of the hurt—and we *still* have to judge. We cannot not judge just because of the hurt that judgment will cause. Instead, we may prepare for it and remember that without judgment we become phony quickly—and our love lacks authenticity and becomes sentimental. We love each other, warts and all, not only once the warts are removed.

I have learned a few tricks of the trade when it comes to judging others. Most of them I learned as a writing teacher. When it comes to judging other people's writing, here is my advice. Always pick out two really good things. Say them first. Then go for the criticism. Use the ratio of two positives to one negative, and the recipients of your advice will grow and grow. Their writing will improve and their trust in you will also improve. People trust our compliments when they also know we are free to be critical with them.

My son sends me letters and has invited me to "criticize" them. He wants help in improving his writing. I just got a letter in which he told the story of giving a cabbie a "fiver" and giving a homeless man an open hand, which "vulnerable fist" the homeless man misinterpreted. I had to tell Isaac that he had done great writing on the "fiver" but was unclear on the "fist." I didn't know what "open hand" or "vulnerable fist" meant. And then, with his permission and encouragement, I had to point out a few clichés. They were not only clichés but also lacking in generosity. He was meeting new people at his summer job and he said they were "boring." Why? Because all they said was "What's your name?" and "Where are you from?" I suggested that he find a better way to say that the so-called newbies were boring. How were they boring? What makes a person boring? Not just the repetition of name and serial number. There is more to it than that. Sometimes when we say that others are boring, what we mean is that we are boring around them. How do we release others? What are some good questions to ask? What is their favorite dance? Why not say something personal to them? That could be fun. When we use catchwords like "boring," we need to be judged, gently, but still judged.

Judgment, generously given, is a form of love and it decreases fear. Under these circumstances, judgment is sacred speech.

6

To Lament

A lament is different from a complaint or a judgment. Complaint carries a ritualized despair, lament a ritualized hope. With a lament we don't necessarily need action—we simply need to speak. There is much in Hebrew Scripture in the form of lament: "My God, my God, why have you forsaken me?" Many of the prose poems of Hosea, where the prophet fears that God has abandoned Israel, are also a "gripe session" elevated. When we lament, we let our hair down and let our trouble out. We don't need a response and don't really expect a response so much as we need to speak. Our utterance is holy by its independence! Like unconditional love, a lament is unconditional. It speaks for the sake of speaking.

A lament can be just a whine or a gripe or a "bitch," in politically incorrect language. It becomes a form of sacred speech to the extent that it adds Spirit to the exposure of the trouble. We speak to Spirit, unconditionally. We don't issue commands, such as telling God not to forsake us. We simply acknowledge that we are forsaken or that we feel forsaken. When we risk a lament, we often do so because of spiritual courage. We may back into this courage because we don't know what else to do—or we may take a conscious risk. A lament is sacred because it liberates. Lament lets pain out of its cage in silence. It is like a good cry—we feel better after it, even though nothing has really changed. Lament trusts Spirit enough to show how awful we feel. We admit trouble to ourselves and to Spirit—and to others who may do us the kindness of listening.

A folklorist named Anna Caraveli studied women's laments in the villages of Greece. According to Caraveli, laments are spontaneous, ritualized oral poems that some Greek women chant to express grief over the loss of loved ones to expatriation or death. Women typically recite laments in the company of other women. Even more significantly, women feel they need other women to participate in the lament for it to be successful. One woman even reported to Caraveli that she could have done it better if she'd had other women there to help her.

A lament differs from a complaint because we don't whine in a lament. We state. We accept. We weep. Complaints are fundamentally despairing kinds of speech. "I can't stand my sister-in-law. Whenever she comes to my house, I get nervous and angry. I can't tell her how I feel—I can't do anything but put up with her unpleasant, judgmental nature. I have no choice." This is a complaint.

A lament ritualizes hope. "I become a person I don't want to be whenever my sister-in-law comes to my house. I become nervous and angry. I have to tell someone how I feel about her and the way she makes me feel small. I know I can't tell her not to come. I know she is a part of my family and that my brother would never forgive me for estranging our kids and families from each other. I have to learn to cope with her." Although there is not a lot of hope in a lament that repositions responsibility for a relationship, there is much more hope than despair. Complaints rant, rave, and air distress. Laments rant, rave, and air distress—and then resolve themselves. We take the next step; we manage some kind of action or at least intend some kind of action.

According to Deborah Tannen, in her popular book *You Just Don't Understand,* women find solace in each other's pain. Many lament, not just women. They tell what hurts and find a spiritual healing in the telling. We find ourselves linked and able to cope once we "tell someone" what is bothering us. The yoke becomes easier, the burden lighter. Secrets are often kept precisely because the pain they carry is too horrible to release. Lament occurs when we trust our partner in conversation enough to express the pain that feels inexpressible. Lament breaks down silence and secrets into speech. We may weep when we tell what we have to tell, but we stop the cold, dry internal tears of bearing burdens alone, in secret. Men also experience great relief in sharing a load, in bringing to light what hurts.

Speech That Carries Spirit

"Evelyn, I haven't wanted to tell you because I knew how upset you would be. I lost my job two weeks ago. The pink slip just showed up on my desk. I have been looking and looking but I haven't found anything yet. I wanted to tell you about the pink slip when I told you about my new job. But I'm not having any luck. How are we going to pay for John's college tuition? What are we going to do? I am so scared. . . ."

This person is going to feel much better now that he and his partner can both bear the load of unemployment. He has opted for trust instead of humiliation. He has accomplished a sacred act in speech: He has told the truth. He has the liberation of lament. As a pastor, it is often my job to encourage people to tell the hard truth of their lives—their unemployment, their adultery, their addiction—to their intimates. They often say they can't, but usually the truth frees them in a way that keeping secrets cages them.

Many people of my generation were raised with the words, "If you can't say anything nice, don't say anything at all." That kind of advice represses speech rather than expresses life. That kind of advice is anti-lament—and therefore against the liberation that the sacred speech of lament offers to people willing to consciously risk it.

After the terrorist attacks of September 11, 2001, my congregation wanted to sing "God Bless America" every week. They wanted the assurance of patriotism, and they also wanted me and the other pastors to back the war that the president initiated. I could manage the singing for a while, and I could even support the necessity of military response. As a pastor, though, I can never support war as a solution to any problem for long. I travel with the "just war" theory and think of violence as a short-term, necessary evil.

When we took "God Bless America" out of the service after six weeks of singing it, there was quite a stir. Did I not support the president? Was I not patriotic? Did I not care about our "boys" across the sea? These comments felt like an attack to me, and they were. They were also a form of lament. "Why can't we all think the same way?"

I responded with my own lament: "Because the truth is that Americans need God's blessing for both our failures and our victories." Very few were in the mood to hear about America's failures. After all, we were innocent victims, ruthlessly attacked. Being a victim, however, does not mean that we are released from the responsibility of living or the responsibility of telling the truth about ourselves. This exchange of lament cleared the air and brought us closer to each other and therefore closer to the truth of our experience under terrorist attack.

> Laments often happen for their own sake rather than for the sake of anything else. They are a release of negative energy in order to make room for a new positive. Laments are complaints reaching for and counting on resolution. Their companion is Spirit. They are directed to Spirit more than to anything else.
>
> Laments hope. Laments open doors. Laments push for reconciliation with the hard reality they express.

It was a painful exchange. We could have lied to each other; I could have pretended to be more patriotic, and that portion of the congregation could have pretended to be less so. But we were both (all, really, as there were many other "sides" as well) in pain. We were reaching for each other with all the strength we could muster—but we were not touching.

Lament lets out the pain. Lament expresses feeling. Lament is holy speech. Life is not all good—and those who trust Spirit know that truth. In lament, we let Spirit aerate conversation.

Sometimes we don't even know that we have a lament to speak. For example, a member of my congregation had left a large bequest to our church in Miami. I had to go to the Bank of America in Atlanta. I went there on "business," the business of her generosity. I went the night before for the 9:00 A.M. appointment and naturally went looking for the location of the bank. I can read, I can drive, and I can plan. Thus I drove up and down Peachtree Street three times looking for number 600. I could not find the Bank of America. That night, after checking into the hotel, I went out on foot. Atlanta has not been nearly as successful as other cities at hiding the homeless downtown, as I had heard from friends who work in churches and shelters there. It was a cold night and the homeless people were everywhere. For a moment, I thought of asking some of them if they knew where the Bank of America was. Then I realized that would be as bad as another mistake I had once made in Philadelphia, when I asked a black man in a grocery line if he knew how to tell whether a watermelon was good. I was just trying to buy one and had it in my hands but wasn't sure. Anyway, I walked down Peachtree Street alone, made friends with some of the locals, and gave out the oranges I had brought with me. Then it happened. I saw deep in a cluster of trees and fountains big numbers reading "600." I looked up. The Bank of America is the tallest building in Atlanta. It was right there. It was just so big I couldn't see it from my little car.

This story tells more about the details of my lament for my country. Great wealth towers over little people. I rarely even know that I fear for the poverty of my country. I only rarely can find the words. I don't want to speak this lament, but I do want banks to be less important and people to be more so.

A good friend of mine tells the story of going to raise money for her antipoverty organization from a banker in a tall building in Manhattan. She paid seventeen dollars to park her car in the lot and went to the thirty-eighth floor. She was successful in getting the grant. When she went back down to the parking lot, she found herself irritated at the man who was getting her car for her. He seemed to be taking forever. Then shame overtook her. She knew that he was not making seventeen dollars an hour. She decided to stop and have a conversation rather than continue what seemed to her to be hypocrisy. "How do you feel about the people whose cars you park all day long?" she asked. He responded, "They can't see us from up there."

This man found a simple way to say a simple lament. He didn't have to say how he felt to this social worker gone self-conscious. He simply had to report a physical fact: "They can't see us from up there." Not being seen is very painful to people who feel invisible. This parking lot attendant did not expect either social change or social justice. He simply spoke of what he saw. He did not generalize. Instead, we heard a simple cry, a powerful, accurate lament that bites to the quick in its description of the reality of poverty.

LAMENT IS A
SPEECH OF HOPE

Very often the quality of our lament over our nation or over poverty is not eloquent. Very often we jeer and complain rather than open ourselves and others to lament. I think of these slogans I saw at a recent demonstration: "Jail for crime in the streets; bail for crime in the suites!" "Stop the gross criminal product." "We are all Enron, we are all Argentina." When we chant these kinds of generalizations, we don't really feel any better. We polarize would-be supporters by lumping people into piles of good and bad. And we utter the speech of despair, rather than the speech of hope.

A lament transcends such generalizations. We know a lament has spoken by its details and its specificity, its beauty, even its willingness to refuse black-and-white thinking. I think in contrast of the slogan of Leon, Nicaragua, left over from the Sandinistas: *Tenemos historeria; hacemos el futuro.*" "We have history; we make the future" is the translation. A lament is marked by its passion for reconciliation.

A lament says a hard thing well. It says the hard thing in a way that leaves the door open for another to move in with us. It does not close doors or use the lateral violence of the insult, even against the people who work high up in the bank, invisibly in charge. A lament gives us and all who listen a way out, an open door at the end of a tunnel.

An ad tells me that a certain kind of automobile company hires mechanics who "stand behind their work." I wish that had been the case at a hotel where I had another embarrassing all-American experience. My family had a reservation for two nights, and on the second night the kids were to have their own room. I called early in the afternoon to confirm, because I knew the hotel was booked solid. Oh, yes, they had a room for the time when all of our children would arrive. When the kids checked in, all they could get was a smoking room with one king-size bed. We of course complained—this was no time for a lament—and at least four people at the front desk told us one of the theme songs of the lesser American. "It is not my fault." "I can do nothing about it." "It is outside of my department."

The story continued. I assumed the kids were in room 625, in the king-size bed and in the smoke. I didn't like it, but I too had become part of that crowd that adopts "there is no alternative" as a point of view. Thus, at midnight, I was looking for the kids in what I thought was their room, banging on the door only to be nearly shot by an unknown gentleman in his boxers. The hotel had done the right thing and moved the kids but not told me.

Sometimes we do the right thing even though we say we can't and it is definitely outside of our department. Sometimes we hear the laments—we even speak the laments—and then we find a way to do the right thing anyway.

Knowing when to speak a lament and when to just complain is a very tricky thing. Complaining or whining is often a spoken form of despair. There is nothing holy about despair. There is something very holy about hope. A genuine lament notes that some banks are so big that they tower over everything and that some poverty is unalleviated. Lament helps us to be unafraid of matters even this large. A complaint is an internalized form of depression. We just rant and rave. We don't control our speech, and we let its sadness be owned by us.

Let me add one more illustration. I had bought a new periwinkle blue silk suit for the appointment at the Bank of America on Peachtree Street. I had it altered a week before I went to Atlanta and picked it up on the way out of Miami. I carried it through the airport, car rental desk, baggage claim, and the like. I put it on a half hour before the meeting only to realize that no work had been done on it whatsoever. The hems of both the pants and the jacket were just as long as they had been when I bought it. Everything else in my bag was sportswear. I wore shorts to the bank meeting and was pretty embarrassed. I was also pretty mad. I had paid the dry cleaner thirty-four dollars plus I had wasted pick-up and delivery time, and he hadn't done his job. This same man had once lost a rug of mine for two months. Because he was kind enough to deliver the rug to me when he found it and did not charge me, I decided to do business with him again. I have a complaint here, not a lament. I no longer have hope that this dry cleaner can do his job.

Why is this important? Like the sociologist of religion who sends two of his four children to church and keeps the other two home on Sundays as a control group, we Americans hedge our bets. We stand behind our work—while not knowing that not everyone else is doing so. Then we set up the issue as "America is either good or bad"—when in fact it is both, not either. I may lament many Americans and their inability to see poverty or do their own jobs. I may lament the "there is no alternative" mindset as a phenomenon because it keeps us from the liberating act of making a hopeful lament. I may be excruciatingly embarrassed as a clergyperson over what is going on with some Roman Catholic priests—but I also smell Vatican III in the air. Trouble can create hope or hopelessness. The sacred speech of lament creates hope. It gives the Spirit a chance to know what bothers us. And it gives us the articulation of our pain. That articulation, especially if disciplined beyond slogans, is liberating.

Whenever I lament what my country has become, I think about people like the donor to our church who had no interest in her own large fortune. She wanted to give it away to the poor. She saw them. Or I think about the many people who do stand behind their work. Or of some of my church members who care for each other in stunning ways.

Or I think of the artists who developed the temporary memorials at the site of the World Trade Center. One memorial consisted of two upward beams of light, at Ground Zero, filling the void in Manhattan's night skyline. The buildings may have been gone, but the light remained and illuminated the emptiness. These lights were sacred speech. They were laments. They cried out over what is no longer there, only to fill it with their own light. The other memorial, Fritz Koenig's "Sphere," may be invited to stay. It is a 27-foot bronze globe, now warped and dented, a survivor of the physical destruction of the place. It too stands, and in the standing, speaks. Sacred speech can be sculptural as well as verbal.

When I think of America and what bothers me about it and how I lament it and love it, I think of my champion son. He is on the world's Frisbee team—and Frisbee is a growing sport, a cross between soccer and football. Jacob excels at this game and has won many honors playing it. When you have a son who is a star, people talk to you differently. I already knew that girls talked to him differently, walked around behind him, ogling. But when we got to the National Frisbee Tournament that year, I could tell that the name of my youngest was in the air. People commended his prowess on the field in competitive terms. Better than So-and-so from Such-and-such. Clearly as good as Such-and-such from Over There. Not as good as Whosis from Wheresis, but then again, he was only a junior.

Then, when they lost the championship to Paideia, a fabulous team from Atlanta, the talk changed. Jacob had tried to do too much. Tried to carry the whole team on his shoulders. Got in the middle of plays he should have stayed out of. Should have understood that if all the defenders were on him, that meant other people were open. Ah, Jacob. To be a star is not easy. You can't do anything right but win. Being a star sometimes means losing the permission to be ordinary. It narrows your options. The rest of us can still fail. You can't.

When it comes to my lament for my country, this star business starts to matter. Like Jacob, America stands on the precipice of arrogance. To be an American is to be a profoundly good and fortunate person who has too much power at his or her disposal. That is my lament. And that is my hope, too. Once we recognize and state our pain, we are on our way to liberation from it.

Lament is the sacred speech that can restore us to hope in ourselves. But we have to be careful of what Jacob experienced on the field. Being a star did not mean he could handle the entire game. If we want to be loved by the rest of the world, we know what to do.

We have to refrain from taking over the whole game ourselves. We have to be excruciatingly careful of slogans and anything that generalizes our nation's pain or goodness. Lament opens up pain when we are specific; it closes down pain and therefore progress when we are inarticulate and overly general.

Lament teaches us what to do with power. We have to expel our power, not hoard it. We have to assume that there is an alternative to the way the powerful want to play the game. We also have to see people in their right size and not look down on them. Lament is a form of sacred speech that is passionate about reconciliation and trusts Spirit to lead us to reconciliation. When we lament, we can say what we see and say where it hurts. Then we can change from being good people who have power standing in their way to good people who got power out of their way.

Patriotic issues are not the only places where lament can be freeing. Neither is woman-to-woman sharing about trouble in relationships the only form of lament that is sacred. Nor is a man confessing that he has lost his job or a woman getting through her dilemma with her sister-in-law. Lament is wide speech and travels the distance among the personal, spiritual, and political.

I think also of prayers and hymns and the way some hymns just help people cry. A famous hymnodist, Brian Wren, says that we "tell the truth through tearful songs."[1] Note that people like to sing these kinds of songs. We like to lament. A good three-hankie movie or worship service goes a long way toward physical and mental well-being. Why? Because it contains the components of lament. There are at least three components. One is hope, a hope that goes beyond complaint or whining. Another is a refusal to generalize and a disciplined insistence on articulation of the real problem, no matter how complex it is. The third is a passion for reconciliation, an open door, a way out.

The reason lament is such a sacred form of speech is that God also uses it. Listen to Shirley Erena Murray's hymn about God and lament. In it we see the pattern of lament.

> God weeps at love withheld, at strength misused, at children's innocence abused and till we change the way we love, God weeps.

> God bleeds at anger's fist, at trust betrayed, at women battered and afraid, and till we change the way we win, God bleeds.

> God cries at hungry mouths, at running sores, at creatures dying without cause, and till we change the way we care, God weeps.

> God waits for stones to melt, for peace to seed, for hearts to hold each other's need, and till we understand the Christ, God waits.[2]

This hymn has all the components of the sacred speech of a lament. It has hope at its heart—it assumes that we will change the way we love, win, and care. It has a general story but is particularly told. And it is passionate about reconciliation. God weeps, bleeds, and waits. In the waiting is the reconciliation.

7

To Love

Love is the holiest of actions. Most religious traditions agree that the force behind creation is God's love and joy in humanity. When we love each other, we imitate the grandest force in creation. We do the "will" and way of God.

Still, love has a hard time being understood. It goes soft and gooey on us when we least expect it. Love is nowhere near "always being nice." Nor is love a sentiment or a feeling by itself; it is also an action with proactive intentionality. The love set loose in creation is unconditional positive regard. It is joy at the other's existence—not approval, but joy.

Speech That Carries Spirit

A mother has three children, two older sons and a daughter. On their eighteenth birthdays, each of the boys hitchhiked across the country, had a wonderful time, and enjoyed the full blessing of his parents. When the daughter turns eighteen, she announces her intention of leaving on her hitchhiking trip. Both parents say absolutely not, that things are different for girls. They have very few double standards, but this one is clear: It is not safe for her to hitchhike across the country. The daughter is as severely disappointed as only an eighteen-year-old can be. Idealism and freedom are attacked in her parents' prohibition.

Then the mother decides to actively love her daughter. "When do we leave?" she asks. The mother joins her daughter on the trip. Not everything is safe for them, nor is it easy. But active love replaces active fear.

As a pastor, I am often consulted on family matters. Almost always the answer to the "question" is to activate love. I hear "But I love him so much" quite a bit, but that is usually beside the point. The issue usually is "How are we going to activate and demonstrate love between us?" Love is not just a feeling. The hitchhiking mother not only loved her daughter in her heart, but she also loved her through her thumb. Sometimes that activation can be sticking to a "no": Some things are not safe, and love protects. Sometimes that activation can be joining a journey a person has to take or joining a mistake a person has to make. Love is not just a feeling or even sacred speech; it is also an action we take to show what we feel. Speech is a method of love, a means to love.

When we speak of love as the primary impulse of creation, we understand that God did not create us so that we would be "good" and please God. God created us to be free. God created us to be ourselves. God let us go in love. When we "say" we love each other, we also need to be able to show unconditional regard for the other's freedom, even the freedom to separate from us, hurt our feelings, or do something we cannot approve.

THE SACRED SPEECH
OF LOVE CAN BE VERY QUIET

Speech That Carries Spirit

One priest in the monastery knew that another priest was extremely depressed. He watched his friend night and day but could find no key to open the joy or gratitude in his heart. Finally, the depressed priest took to his bed and wouldn't get out of it. No amount of cajoling worked. The priest who was his friend lay down on the bed next to him and stopped talking. His only words as he began this afternoon ritual were "I am with you here." The friend stayed an hour every day and then went about his business. On the fiftieth day, the depressed man got up and went to Mass. His healing was accomplished by the act of loving companionship. Many words had failed before the "I am with you here" had worked.

Love at its best is "I am with you here." I am not here to change you, improve you, educate you, use you, manipulate you, control you, or benefit from you. I am with you here. Love is not instrumental. It does not make of itself anything but what it is. That's why we speak of God's love as unconditional love, a love that is beyond conditionality.

Many sages argue that there is nothing we can do or fail to do that will alter God's love for us. That kind of love is ours when we rise above conditions and find a way to be present to each other, without instrumentation.

I think of a mother whose five-year-old emphatically told her she would no longer be needing the training wheels on her bicycle. The mother doubted but decided the best thing to do was to see. She removed the training wheels on the bike. The daughter sped away. As she cycled out of sight—for the first time in her mother's or her own life—her mother wept tears of joy that were also tears of sorrow. She saw what it meant to let someone go—and she knew that was the job of a parent.

God's love is like this mother's love. God's love for us is not only capable of saying yes or no, of being present or absent, as the priest was present nonjudgmentally, as the hitchhiking mother was present judgmentally. God's love also lets us go. It even lets us fall off a bicycle or two.

I want to use this framework of the training wheels as a way of talking about different kinds of love. Surely the love of a parent for a child is elemental and biological at its base. Most of us love our blood relatives. In a way, that kind of love, with its heavy economic and biological support, is three-wheeler kind of love. It is tricycle love. We get a lot of support from our bodies and our checkbooks and our culture when we love a member of our family, particularly when a parent loves a child. Training-wheel love, that first step of the two-wheeler, is another kind of love. It is more adolescent in nature and has to do with loving those who are our friends but not our relatives. And two-wheeler love, which glides into maturity, is blissfully capable of loving ourselves as well as our blood relatives and our friends. It is from this mature love and appreciation of self that we are capable of a higher kind of spiritual love, love for our neighbor, a stranger, the undeserving, and even the unknown.

The Jewish law of *tzedakah* comes into play here. The lowest order of morality is understood to be care of our blood relatives. The highest is care of those we don't even know, the kind of charity that donates to a symphony or builds a new building on a college campus. In between there are gradations of friendship and adoption. When we think of sacred speech as love, we are thinking of the entire spectrum. We are thinking of the friendship of two priests who care for each other even after one becomes ill. We are thinking of the unselfishness of (most) mothers who do let their children go off on their own. And we are thinking of a language that is very hard to put into "big" words. Better words for love are the smaller ones, the detailed ones, the ones that reach for affirmation of the other.

My husband and I were in Atlanta for a kids' weekend sports event and had spent the whole day at the field. The kids weren't back yet, so we took a late afternoon walk through a huge parking lot next to our motel. He said, "Must be a corporation in this lot here somewhere." I said, "Duh," implying that he was stupid. Or rather, that I was smarter and would never be caught saying something so obvious.

Love skips opportunities to go one up. Instead of taking the opportunity to proclaim my intelligence, I might instead have said, "Do you think so?" or something neutral. In my heart I could say "Duh" all I wanted, but in my speech I could have found a better way. In intimate relationships, there are constant opportunities to compete with one another. When we refuse those opportunities and instead reach for the other in speech, we do something sacred with our tongue.

Examples abound of family love or love that brings us rewards of an emotional or a financial nature. In this kind of basic, tricycle love, we run many risks. Let's just focus on two of the most common risks in tricycle, or biological family, love. They will prepare us for sacred speech. They are the sin of pride—the overdoing, the over-functioning, the overachievement—and the sin of sloth, the underdo-ing, the underfunctioning, and the spiritual laziness of not grabbing hold of one's life. These are time-honored sins and they have these modern labels, both derived from our machine age. We "burn out" because we crank the engine too often. Or we rust out because we crank the engine too infrequently. How exactly are we to know which is which?

Love in the family is always reaching for proportion, for right-sized living. Harry Stack Sullivan, the great theorist of education, said, "Learning is the organization of experience." When we love in the family, we need to get the size of our spiritual clothing right. Consider this book to be a spiritual fitting.

Parents can love their children too much. They can hurt them by being too attached to them or by living through them. Parents can also neglect their children. They can give too little security or atten-tion, and children can suffer from it. Likewise, sibling issues can pre-sent extraordinary opportunities for the sacred speech of love, as well as extraordinary risks. It is no accident that the Greeks made great tragedy out of Oedipus and many less famous siblings.

Speech That Carries Spirit

My twins, Katie and Jacob, were at an event where my son's girl-friend, a former close friend of my daughter's, was present. The triangle was superbly framed. Katie wanted Jacob to "be with her" at this youth event. Jacob wanted to be with his girlfriend. Katie snarled and became very jealous. Then came the trouble:

The twins would not be together for their birthday, so at this event Katie gave Jacob a very carefully chosen birthday gift, a book of photography by her favorite artist. His girlfriend was present as the gift was given. "That looks more like a present for Katie than a present for Jacob," she said knowingly, professing an intimacy that might have warmed everyone had it not been for the previous jealousy. Katie was really hurt. For her, sacred speech in this little family-plus-one was to state honestly, "That really hurts me, Cathy." She was breaking out of her pique back into her friendship with both of her friends. She was saying how important each was to her, as well as noting how important it was that they not only know her but receive her gifts with gladness. Cathy was able to say another form of loving sacred speech: "Oh, Katie, I am so sorry! I didn't mean to hurt your feelings. I didn't know all that you were feeling." Cathy did know that Katie was jealous, and thus she was able to correct her peccadillo of fostering Katie's fear of being distanced from her brother.

These are not big words. These are small words. This is not a big incident. It is a small one. But love shows its colors in the small stuff.

IS LOVING SPEECH NAÏVE?

There are some people who simply have to correct everything another person says. They exist in almost every family. Sacred speech prefers not to bother with correction. Sacred speech tries to find what it can agree with and then move on. There is a simple, nearly naïve optimism to sacred speech. It assumes it can get along with just about anybody, including a relative who is difficult. How? It says yes to the other in every way imaginable.

I remember the courtship years with my husband very fondly. The thing I loved most about them was the way he said yes to just about everything I said. He had a deep sense of yes for me in him. As we have matured and gone beyond the training-wheel stage of love, where we have had to manage more data and diapers together than either of us could ever have imagined, we have both journeyed forward to another kind of love. We don't say yes to each other all the time. In the larger yes that we have said, in our marriage covenant, there is room for other kinds of love. In courtship we are often wearing the training wheels of sex, youth, romance, and all the rest. Just because this is an early stage of love does not mean that it is not magnificent! Rather, it is buoyed up by supports we can't count on to last forever.

While blood-relative love may be the most basic kind of love, it is nonetheless also capable of being the most difficult. It is in the family that most of us say the most unholy things. Fussing is a hobby of most families—but it does not get what we really want from our families, which is a certain security and comfort. We want a sense of yes. We want to be heard in the affirmative. We want to be listened into speech. My advice to myself, frequently, is simply to fake the yes even when I don't feel it. I'm not kidding. I think there is truth to behavior modification. I know how to act as though I am interested in what you are saying. Often that "act" brings us out far enough into the clearing of our relationship that I *become* interested, when I wasn't before, just by virtue of what you say—if I am open to hearing it. There is a relational quality to speech. We interact while speaking. We draw each other out, and then we can hear each other. Or we close each other down, and then we can't.

No less a sage than Thomas Aquinas, in the *Summa Theologica,* defends affability and cheerfulness. When it comes to modifying our behavior toward love, affability can go a long way. Aquinas actually takes to task people who are so serious about themselves that they never say anything ridiculous. *Nec ipsi dicunt aliquid ridiculum!* If we can't find a way to engage another in the family with something positive or affirming, sometimes resorting to the witty can help.

In my family, for instance, you might hear an exchange like this: "Please put on some more sunscreen, I have asked you a thousand times." "Mom, you get to mention the sunscreen, skin cancer, the ozone layer, and imminent death four more times on this trip to the beach. The fifth time I steal your water bottle."

People who do not befriend the ridiculous but instead are always trying to obstruct the fun or amusement of others are morally unsound, in Thomas Aquinas's opinion. "Bear yourself with wit," he advises, "lest you be regarded as sour or despised as dull."

Nimbleness of wit has long been considered an authentic virtue. Aristotle called it *eutrapelia,* or a happy turn of mind. I was astonished to read the following commentary by Thomas Aquinas concerning the fourth book of Aristotle's ethics. Thomas was not slim. *Grossus et brunus* were two of the adjectives used to describe him. Remigio, his student in Paris, didn't hesitate to describe his famous master as a very fat man indeed. Thomas, in his commentary on Aristotle's ethics, says, "Those who are small might be called pretty because of an appropriateness of color and a fitting proportion of the limbs. However, they cannot be called beautiful because of a lack of magnitude." In other words, thin people can be pretty, but beautiful people have substance. Let the Latin amuse you: *Pulcritudo proprie consistit in corpore magno* ("Beauty is found in a large body").[1]

Love is unconditional positive regard and imitates how God feels about us. It is the reason God made us. Love has levels, biological and beyond. We find the most sacred of words—and sometimes the most difficult—in the act of loving each other. Two guides can help us the most. One is to keep our speech positive and reaching, without being dishonest about what hurts us. The other is wit: We can be funny in many ways.

In families, we are connected to each other's bodies. We say things about each other's bodies that should really rarely be said, such as "Who farted?" in a small car on a trip. We wouldn't say these things "outside." There is a sacred character to these intimacies—and there is also danger in them. Most of us want to be truly known as much as we want to be truly loved.

A psychiatrist told me that he said to a beautiful young model hooked on Quaaludes, "I don't get it. You have everything in the world going for you. You make tons of money. You are on everyone's A list for openings and sold-out events. Men throw themselves at your feet. Yet you seem to be doing everything in your power to destroy yourself. What gives?"

The beautiful model responded, "What gives is the garbage you just spewed. All you see is the outside, my beauty. An accident of birth is why you're talking to me. Would you pay attention to a stoned woman who was ugly? And you're so impressed with all the things I have access to, but do you know me?"

Happiness is being role-free. Happiness is being status-free. Family is a role- and status-free place—where we are constantly trying to insert roles and status. How do we keep family familial or grace graceful? From knowledge that nothing can separate us, or our flesh, perfect or imperfect as it may be, from the love of God. Families exist to express the unconditional love of God.

Sometimes we succeed and sometimes we fail. Two guides can help us the most. One is to keep our speech positive and reaching—without being dishonest about what hurts us. The other is wit: We can be funny in families in many ways.

THE SPEECH OF FRIENDSHIP

When we move out of family speech to the speech of friends, we move into equally dangerous territory. Love is not only the best thing. It is also the most dangerous thing, whether we are in tricycle- or training-wheel stages or riding a mountain bike a thousand miles through the Rockies. These metaphorical supports are just ways to understand the stages and conditions of love. In friendship, we choose our friends—and thus apply conditions to them. These conditions are like training wheels. Perhaps the friends went to our school. Maybe they like the same food that we do. We may enjoy going out with athletes or with people who appreciate classical music.

In friendships, we find ourselves in need of all the skills we can get—the skills of vulnerability, reaching for positive connections, and wit. We also find ourselves learning a new skill—the art of self-revelation. What makes someone a really good friend is that he or she wants to know who we are and is willing to listen. "She listens with the same attention most people reserve for speaking." That is the mark of a good friend. "We hear each other into speech" is the way the feminist slogan puts it.

Friends do well to ritualize relationships—to always have Thanksgiving together or to have certain games that are played over time. When we ritualize relationships, we create structure for the important hearing and reviewing of each other's lives. We make defined space for the sacred speech of telling each other who we are.

Speech That Carries Spirit

We are holding a mistake contest in our office. Every year at the holiday party we give an award to the person who made the best mistake during the past year. Last year, the winner was the typo in the first line of the stewardship letter. The year before that, it was nearly electrocuting the photographer who was doing the photo directory. He survived. So did our pledge campaign. But we had doubts all the way. Ritualizing such mistakes at a staff party lets coworkers be friends—as well as saying that the lines are clear. We are now forgiven and on "forward," not perpetual "rewind."

Love as friendship only improves when it moves through conflict. Many people know the blessing of a conflict safely passed—and it makes their friendships and families stronger. Sacred speech is necessary to get us from one moment to the next. We learn the art of conflict in both families and friendships.

One man in my parish couldn't stop referring to the wonderful qualities of the previous pastor while in my presence. I finally told him that it was like being the new wife and always hearing that the deceased was better in bed. He got the point. He stopped. Why didn't I say something the first time? Why do I wait out trouble as though growing it to full term will somehow help the matter?

Both work relationships and friendships have conditions. We will stay friends as long as we have fun together. We will work together as long as we do the job we have been assigned and to which we have committed. In friendships and in work relationships, sacred speech carries risks—and the risks carry grace. In love, we tell people who we are. We tell people we know we have made a mistake, and we get to move on.

I think of Carol Gilligan telling the story of a girl she was interviewing. The girl was twelve, right at that age where Gilligan has shown many girls shut down and start being and doing what their culture tells them to be and do. The girl said to Gilligan, "Do you want me to tell you what I think? Or do you want me to tell you what I really think?"

Some working relationships and friendships are not safe enough for truth. Sacred speech has a character of fundamental freedom and lack of fear. When we find that we cannot say what we really think, we probably should move out of the relationship, if at all possible. We are creatures of God, not creatures of culture or paycheck or status. But if we can't move out of the relationship, as we sometimes can't move out of a family, then we resort to the family virtues of affability, affirmation, and wit. There is nonviolence to sacred speech, which wagers that it will be the last loving one on the field when the whole game is over.

Speech That Carries Spirit

"Rebecca, your work continues to be below the level we have in this office," said the manager. "When I started working here four years ago, Ms. Roberts," said Rebecca, "I was filing twelve claims a day. Now I am filing thirty-five. I am doing the best I can. You can be sure that I will try to do better." Sometimes all we can do is agree with our "persecutor." But we don't have to say much more than our truth. Numbers, like Rebecca's, can help. Sticking to the facts almost always helps, as does returning the complaint to the complainer with an intention to improve.

The most mature kind of love is when we love people we don't even know. We might call it two-wheeler love. This kind of love is the least supported of all. We rarely get paychecks or rewards for it. We rarely get reimbursed emotionally or otherwise. There are no expense accounts attached to mature love. But we are called to do it all the time.

The Russian poet Pushkin, who was often quoted by Sakharov, the Russian scientist and dissident who gave up his home and his life for the ideal of freedom, put it this way:

And long by the people will I be loved
For I have struck the chords of kindness
And sung freedom's praise in this cruel age
Calling for mercy to be shown the fallen.

Finally, there is no doubt that some of the most sacred words are used in hospitals, places where often there isn't much that can be said. Amid pain, despair, boredom, loud and constant noise, and staff overload, many nurses find their way to say, "I know, honey, I know." Some even show up after the call button has been blinking for forty-five minutes, touch an elderly patient's hand, and say, "I can't help you now, I wish I could, I'll get here as soon as I can." As more than one patient will happily tell you, these words can mean as much as getting a diaper change. Kindness is a form of love, and the world aches for it, in Stalinist regimes and in room 403. This kind of love will not get rewarded by the nursing supervisor or the president. Its reward is itself.

Tricycle love gives us families, connection, and help with the mortgage. Training-wheel love gives us friends and the chance to become an individual, a self. Two-wheeler love gives us choices and responsibilities and helps make life joyful and good. Love beyond support of even the wheels is the most sacred and is not in competition with the others. Instead, that love is the guide and goal.

8

Beyond the Politically Correct

Sacred speech has a quality of truth to it, even if the truth is hard. Sacred speech is less "correct," which is another version of righteousness or truth, than it is honest and authentic. A new catchphrase has crept into our vocabulary, and it tells us a lot about the pollution of language and words. The catchphrase is "politically correct." By it we mean that the person is reaching for the truth but doing so in a way that bothers us. We know the difference between the correct and the truthful. The truth contains or reaches for love; the correct contains or hides fear. Being correct is just a way to stay out of trouble with perceived authorities; being true is a matter of staying and being free.

The catchphrase "politically correct" is like many slogans. It has enough truth to bear repetition and enough falsehood to bear watching. Sometimes we make racist comments, inadvertently or not, and when someone calls us on it by saying we have made a "racist" comment, the first line of defense is to accuse the one who has judged us. We say, "You are being politically correct," implying that we were not wrong in whatever we said or did.

"I was so scared that night on Miami Beach on Memorial Day weekend when everyone on the boardwalk and the beach was black and I was the only white person." So said my daughter at her seventeenth birthday party, in front of two of her friends and me. All of us are white. I doubt she would have said it if one of us were black. She wouldn't have wanted to be seen noticing color. However, she was scared and she did express it. Is she politically incorrect? I think not. But had I said this, I can imagine one of my friends saying to me, "Why are you so color alert?" We grew up in the '60s and coined the politically correct reactions.

Political correctness is playing games. It is a cul-de-sac of speech. We paint ourselves into a corner when we accuse someone else of being politically correct. We use an excuse to cover up a gaffe—and next thing we know we are cornered by our own linguistic inadequacy. It is no wonder that many people feel angrily silenced by "politically correct speech." They are accurately reflecting what happens when we paint ourselves into a corner. Think of it literally—we have a door, but we apply wet paint between us and it. Once we defend ourselves by accusing another of falsely accusing us—"you are being too politically correct"—we have no place to go in the relationship. We are at the end of the road. We can't apologize for what we may have done wrong, nor can our friend reach out to us in forgiveness. The conversation is over.

In sacred speech, we keep the doors open. Sacred speech is an act of love that overcomes fear. It is always looking for the doors and windows, always looking for the fresh air in speech. When we either accuse someone or receive the accusation of being "politically incorrect," the thought police have entered the room. We have nowhere to go when someone else is controlling our mind and our speech. We shut down. That is the work of the devil in metaphoric terms. There is no way out.

In sacred speech, we keep doors open for ourselves to use and we keep doors open for others to use. Imagine if I or one of Katie's white friends had said to her after she made her honest admission of fear, "Can't you just wait for the time when we don't have to pay attention anymore to which color the crowd is on the beach?" Katie would have then been reminded that she is "colorizing" an experience, often a preamble to racism, while not being humiliated that she has expressed her feelings.

Sacred speech opens doors. Sacred speech works for love. It gives people a "way out" of a mistake, as opposed to boxing them in. Sacred speech has a fairly constant level of forgiveness to it. Sacred speech is secure enough in the Spirit that it doesn't need to be afraid—either of speaking wrongly or of being so accused. Sacred speakers are secure enough to make mistakes and sure enough of forgiveness to open their mouths around difficult subjects such as race.

Sacred speakers live in a world that is free and secure. There are thought police, but we don't pay attention to them. They have nothing to say to us that we have to hear. Politically correct people are playing games with the thought police and then playing games with us. They choose to pacify the thought police rather than praising God. At its root, the mistake is a spiritual one—and like many spiritual mistakes, it has its own consequences. We wind up living at the end of a road, painted into a room. There are no doors or windows. Our fear has won the day.

I remember what happened to the TV show titled *Politically Incorrect*. In the fall of 2001, Bill Maher, the host, called the American military cowardly for fighting its wars with remote-control cruise missiles and implied that the terrorists of September 11th were comparatively brave for dying and being direct in their attacks. The ABC network canceled the program. Ironic, isn't it, that a show designed to open doors and windows in closed rooms, if ever too irreverent, would be canceled for doing what it was supposed to do?

Patriotism is sacred speech as long as people can differ. When people can only praise their country, that praise is perfunctory and politically correct. The thought police have won. Those of us who doubt that there is any bravery whatsoever in suicide bombings don't have to be silenced when we fear that ABC is in charge of patriotism. They have made a mistake. It is a sacred mistake. True patriots praise and criticize their country. They are free to do so. Speech that is not free is not sacred; it is unholy. Sacred speech stills fear and releases love. Freedom is essential for love.

Truly free speech can ramble without a destination. Politically correct speech is always thinking of what it can say without getting into some kind of trouble. Free speech rambles openly in a world that is free.

SPEECH WITH SPIRIT
LISTENS TO SPIRIT

Free speech and sacred speech travel the way and lean toward truth. They stay on the road. Classical Taoist philosophy, as formulated by Lao-tzu (circa sixth century B.C.E.) and Chuang-tzu (third century B.C.E.), was a reinterpretation and development of an ancient Chinese belief in a well-integrated and unified cosmos. Lao-tzu and Chuang-tzu, living at a time of social disorder and great religious ferment that challenged the notion of a unified or integrated cosmos, developed the notion of Tao, which means "a way" or "a path." By this term they meant something leading out from the origin of all creation, which will continue to the destiny of all creation. It is a force unknowable in its essence but observable in its manifestations.

Sacred speech is like this open ramble: It follows the way. It follows the path. It does not do what it is told by any human being. It does do what it is "told" by following the Spirit. In following the path, sacred speech finds in its manifestations that the world is open, that there are doors and windows. We don't know that the world is open until we open our mouths! The very opening of our mouths opens the world and the way and the path. The closing of our mouths closes the way and the path. We don't know the positive manifestations of sacred speech until we speak, nor do we know the negative manifestations when we are silenced by political correctness.

The early Taoists taught the art of living and surviving by conforming to the natural way of things. They called their approach to action *wu-wei*. Such action is modeled on nature, especially the free flow of water. Sacred speech exists in a world that is natural, free, created. Unholy speech or politically correct speech exists in a world that is closed and governed by mortals who have "agendas," who play games, who think they are the way rather than knowing that all we can do is follow the way.

One game people love to play is the game of control. We set the goal of self-control rather than God's control. We don't tell everything we know, and we set each other up. Or we insert negativity at just the right moment so that the conversation turns down when it might have built up. We whine. Or we go over and over the same territory as though we wanted our side to win some presumed lifelong war. We are nervous without the war, so in order to keep our anxiety controlled, we re-skirmish where skirmishes could be over. Without the war, we'd have to go on with our life. Keeping the war going means we won't have to do much that is courageous or noble. We don't have to play or have fun. We have the skirmish as an excuse.

When some of my very good friends became "politically correct" in their speech and behavior, when almost everything that happened was accused of having racism or sexism at its foundation, I realized that these friends were not able to give up on the '60s. They were hanging on to the old skirmish on behalf of their own power and control. Again, I am not saying that racism and sexism don't exist; both do, in unfortunate plenty. But abolishing them is an act of love and of opening doors and windows, not an act of control and closing the air out of conversation. From either the right or the left, politically correct people shut down conversation. Sacred speech opens up the flow.

As Stokely Carmichael said, "Racism is not my fault, but it is my responsibility." Racism continues to exist precisely because we don't find nonviolent ways to stop it. The thought police and the politically correct people have done as much to prolong racism as to stop it: They have painted people into corners when their loving task should have been to paint them a way out.

Sacred speech imitates divine behavior. Spirit is always opening the way forward, the way out, the way through. That is the Tao, and we follow it. We do not lead the Tao or make the Tao; we follow it. We should seek reconciliation at every turn, even if that involves loving our enemies or being good to those who hurt us. It is not virtuous to hate racists, and it is not virtuous to hate sexists. Neither is it virtuous to hate people we think are insufficiently patriotic. Hate is not sacred speech. Love is. Love opens and follows the Tao, while hate always knocks us off the path.

Vivian Paley has written a very interesting book called *You Can't Say You Can't Play.* She thinks that some children can learn better in play than they can in reading class. In particular, kids who have a hard time reading and learning in traditional ways need to be taught in the schoolyard, rather than in the classroom. The one rule she says is absolute with young kids is that they are required to return to the circle if they walk out. They have to try again. They may not be allowed to remove themselves from the game. Paley's research indicates that kids who are required to stay in the game also teach themselves how to learn and how to read. Kids who quit to sit on the sidelines stop learning how to learn.[1]

Adults have the same experience with games. We quit and don't even know we have quit. We think we are still fighting the good fight against racism when in fact we are just being angry all the time. We aren't stopping racism—we are adding to its pile of hate. Or we stop learning how to manage a difficult job or relationship because we have one too many curveballs thrown at us. We take our ball and go home. Maybe we aren't sitting on the porch with an actual ball in our lap, but we are no longer on the playing field. Instead, we are playing another game, the game of self-protection, the game of hedged bets, the game of personal control. We stop the reign of God on behalf of the game. We detour from the Tao. And we stay closed to the possibility of reconciliation rather than opening ourselves to it.

God agrees: You can't say you can't play. We imagine we can hide from God's promises or from each other or from difficulty. We hide in the corners into which we paint ourselves. There we imagine that we can be safe by accusing others of what we are not. Sacred speakers know there is no need to hide. There is no need to self-protect. There is no need to be afraid.

If you are someone who has left a meeting or a family dinner or a staff session in hard, cold tears, saying something like, "I am sick of playing games," listen in to the promise of Spirit, the promise of the way. If you have had to swear to someone recently that you are the right kind of patriot and someone else is the wrong kind, listen in on the speech of God. It is certain. It is comprehensive, bravely refusing to differentiate between the right kind of patriot and the wrong kind. Fresh ideas are even now being revealed; before they appear, God shows them. "Behold," God says to the person in the hall who is sick of games, sidelined by life, "behold, I am doing something new. Can you see it? Take one more step. Now can you see it?"

> Truly sacred speech has less interest in pleasing others than it has in pleasing God. Its destination is the truth, not the correct. It has internal judges that matter, making external judges still important but not ultimately important. Politically correct speech paints people into corners, closes doors and windows, and is too arrogant to be sacred.

A friend told me his favorite description of a good preacher. "That preacher could tell his people to go to hell and they would look forward to the trip." I've always wanted to be the kind of preacher who would dare people to go to Heaven, not threaten them with hell. If we have to tell someone that he or she has said something "racist," we can do so by opening doors, not by accusation.

In the situation with my daughter, for instance, I could have said, "Listen, Katie, I am really uncomfortable when I hear you notice the color of rowdy people who made you afraid. Why did you feel you had to say they were black? Tell me more about why. I know you're not a racist, and I realize that you were scared over there on the beach. Tell me more."

If we cannot find our way to sacred speech or to open doors when another's speech has made us uncomfortable, we can simply "defect in place," a great slogan used by feminists, courtesy of Allison Stokes, to describe the behavior of what women do in church while we await justice there.

Our friend Macy was five years old when Katie was sixteen. Macy said to Katie, "Can you come over to my house now? We could play dress up. I have lots of clothes. Go, Katie, go ask your mom." Katie had not asked her mom for permission to play dress up for a long, long time. Can you see God in Macy's playful invitation? Do you see the fresh new part of it? Come, one bigger than I, come to my house. And play. Play dress up. Let us make believe we can be anyone we want to be. Can you come out to play today? God said you can. You don't really have to ask for more permission. The rules are fair; God guaranteed. Just get back, joyfully, into the game.

God is in charge, not us. The reign of God is already here. There is grace at the bottom of justice. We don't have to make it so much as receive it, playfully, confidently, happily.

Reinhold Niebuhr wrote a prayer about arrogance, which is the heart of the problem in politically correct speech.

God forgive us our virtues.
Tis they more than our sins
That sear the heart
Till in imperious disdain
We stand from all our kind apart
Not from age old cruelties
Which we all openly confess
Has ever flowed such endless woe
As from our ruthless righteousness.[2]

HYPOCRITICAL SPEECH

Politically correct speech paints people into corners, closes doors and windows, and is too arrogant to be sacred. If that were not enough to close the case, we also have to deal with the sheer hypocrisy of it. When we accuse another of a political sin, we act as though we were finally redeemed from it. As a recovering racist and a recovering sexist, I know that is not true of me. I would have gone to that beach and noticed color that night. And I am a graduate as well as a teacher of dozens of antiracism training programs.

The hypocrisy of politically correct speech is its worst feature. I think of Camille Paglia's book, *Sexual Personae: The Upper World and the Lower World*, in which she argues that sex today seems open but in actuality is not—that as liberated as we think we are in matters of the body and its many pleasures, we still have a lot of underground through which we trek, in and out of relationships. Are these troubles sins? Yes, they are. It is a sin not to take joy in the body, sexually. Even the Puritans thought so. Our creation includes sexuality. We miss the mark of our creation when we step outside the boundary or trespass on God's intention of joy for us. Love and passion and sexuality are gorgeous parts of our creation. Many of us trespass by missing the mark of joy in relationship.

Nor is it only people in relationships who have trouble with their sexuality. On Valentine's Day, my e-mail messages were full of jokes in which singles refer to their missing partnerships. I love the country song roundup where a woman asks, "Did I shave my legs for this?" Her disappointment in matters of the flesh is keen. And the song "Don't Put Me in the X-Files" is very popular. Why? Because so many of us have been left behind by so many! "You Can't Have Your Kate and Edith Too" refers to the continuing problem of people who think that one partner is just not enough for them. Another song is "Your Negligee Has Turned to Flannel." And then there is the problem of people who stay married but stop liking each other, exemplified in the tune, "You're the Reason Our Kids Are So Ugly." Many of us don't intentionally fast from the pleasures of the flesh—instead, we fast unintentionally. Many people are actually starving for love and touch and pleasure in a world that is absurdly oversexualized.

Too many of us declare ourselves free and open—and live lives that are closed and judgmental and lonely. Politically correct language is not only trespassing on Spirit and on the way; it is also "trash-passing." Trash-passing moves emotional garbage through the system: it continues the dishonesty and the hurt. We fake what should be true.

Trespassing and trash-passing disregard the way of Spirit in the name of control and power of the self. In Greek mythology, Prometheus is one of the Titans, a race of gods who inhabited the earth before the creation of humanity. When the Olympians, another group of gods, fought the Titans, Prometheus sided with Zeus, who wanted to be chief of the gods. After the war, Zeus gave Prometheus and his brother the job of recreating all the living creatures, animal and human, that were killed during the war. Prometheus wanted to ensure that human beings would be superior to all the animals and thought that if people could have some of the sacred fire from Mount Olympus, their survival and superiority would be maintained. Zeus forbade it, claiming, "The fire is for the gods alone." This is almost exactly what Jesus said to the devil on the mountain. Still Prometheus couldn't bear seeing his creations shivering in the cold and eating raw meat, so he stole fire from the gods. What made the theft worse than a mere defiance was that it unleashed an enormous creativity in human beings. Culture and literacy among mortals is said to have developed because of Prometheus's stubborn pride. Just watch the flesh tighten its grip on our spirits. I, for one, want both culture and literacy and to walk humbly with my God. I want power and passion while not being idolatrous. I want to be politically correct in a humble way. I want power on my path, but just a little less than the gods have.

As punishment for his defiance, Prometheus was chained to a rock atop Mount Caucasus, where he was helpless against the elements. Zeus's ultimate penalty was to send an eagle to tear his flesh and eat his liver every day. I know it's a stretch, but I think the small, nonstop difficulties I have with my computer are like having my liver torn out every day (not to mention my near addiction to E-mail). Like Icarus, many of us get burned for flying too close to the sun. We don't manage our passions well. I daresay most of us would agree that culture and literacy are too marvelous for us. We have yet to make a world of joy and peace and justice. Instead, hypocrisy reigns, well defended by politically correct speech.

Obviously, I have set up a problem that I cannot personally solve. The problem is human passion and human power. Jesus solved it by saying no to the devil. Prometheus solved it by saying yes to his pride. Notably, both of them were pecked at in a wilderness. And both of them argue for the abundant virtue in humanity—Jesus arguing that we can transform ourselves by love; Prometheus, that we can read and write and think and master. Inside these enormous pleasures and freedoms, why should we not accuse others who are less committed to a gender-neutral and race-neutral world? What keeps us on the path? What keeps us from digressing and trespassing the path? What myths do we live by?

Trespassing is a world-class sin. Trash-passing is amateur stuff. Trespassing is believing your pride when your pride says you are in charge of plutonium, quarks, air travel, your teenagers, your health, your computer, your swimming pool filter. Trespassing steals too much of the fire from Mount Olympus. Trash-passing is trivializing the passions involved in living. Trash-passing is indulging in politically correct rhetoric. Trash-passing is putting in a strip mall where something sacred belongs. It's littering, or smoking behind your partner's back or behind the school in a back alley. Trash-passing is the little stuff that many of us do when no one is looking. We think it won't hurt anybody. It will.

My son went to a demonstration against globalization in New York City and saw a sign, "We are all either Enron or Argentina." When I asked him what it meant, he said he didn't know. That is trash-passing. Believing someone else's sign that simplifies the enormity of the effects of globalization is trash-passing. It is wobbly thinking, badly thrown about, and silence too often accompanies it. "Well, I didn't want to say anything. . . ."

Leadership, by the way, is the ability to complete passes, good throws well caught. In many conversations, we have incomplete passes. That incompletion is also trash-passing. Leaders learn how to use sacred speech, how to maximize love and how to minimize fear. We aren't born knowing how; we learn.

Recently the county commissioners called me about the invitation I had already accepted to say an invocation at one of their meetings. The call was to advise me on the content. "Your invocation should be under five minutes, nondenominational, and not say anything about God or Jesus." I understand about Jesus. But the idea that I would not bring up God in an invocation strikes me as a trashpass. It is a trespass against my ordination and my role as someone who prays to ask me not to bring up God. In a way, that's what Prometheus did. Could he have initiated art and science in the world and not offended Zeus? Can these things not be for the glory of God? Did Jesus have to say such a loud no to the devil? Wasn't there some room for compromise? I think not. Jesus thought not. When it comes to who is God and who is "man," in the old term—who is "human" in the new term—when it comes to who is God and who we are, there is no room for compromise. To paraphrase Ken Kesey, you are either on the bus or off the bus. As a Taoist would say, you are either on the path or off the path.

Comedian Lily Tomlin says, "If love is the answer, could someone remind me what is the question?" The question is lifelong remembering who and whose we are. It is staying on the path and not getting seduced off it by our own or another's trespassing behavior. The question is human power and passion. The answer is that God loves us—even more than Zeus loved Prometheus—and that we may also love and honor God with our power and our passion. God made us to speak freely and truthfully. Our hypocrisies will not protect us.

What is true about rambling, open discussion along life's way is that we rarely have all the answers. Politically correct language is a near impossibility—on both small and large matters.

When a church member named John asked me about tranquility, at the end of the coffee hour one Sunday, he was six months away from death, or maybe less, according to his doctor. Lung cancer, we all knew, was going to take him soon. John wanted to know why some people have a personal relationship with God and others, like him, do not.

He said he wanted "no more days." He was seventy-something, tired, whipped. He still made it to church almost every Sunday, and sometimes his oxygen tank buzzer went off during the prayers. I thought of the tank as intercessory: Keep John alive. Give John air. Keep him going. Please.

Most of the time, though, both he and it were very quiet.

After church that Sunday, he asked me about peace and tranquility. He wanted to be free of worry about his wife, Charlotte, whom he loved with all his heart. He had taken care of her and her bad knees for years. Now the roles were reversed and he wasn't so sure he could stand to see her manage. She was managing well. He was still worried.

I fumbled around. "So love is robbing you of tranquility," I said. He, being the oppositional type, said no, that's not it.

"So what is it?" I said. "Is it about Heaven?"

"No, that doesn't bother me."

"Is it about pain?"

"No, pain is pain."

"Is it about. . . ." Before I finished my last fumble, he said with vigor that resulted in a coughing fit, *"I don't know what it's about and that is the problem."* When he finished coughing, he said, "It's about tranquility."

"It's about tranquility," I repeated, mostly because I didn't know what else to say.

Deep in a fumble, I remembered these practices called "verbatims." While training for ministry we had to record, to the best of our ability, every word the patient said and every word we said. Then the supervisor would read them and show us how ridiculous we were.

I sincerely hoped no supervisor ever got hold of this conversation.

So far, I had completely managed not to understand John, who was asking me some very simple spiritual questions. Yet, I knew what he wanted, and I even knew why he wanted it. And I also knew why he couldn't have it.

He really didn't have a personal relationship with God, and thus genuine suspicion blocked his peace. Also, he deeply loved his life and partner and family, and he worried about leaving them and them leaving him. That was what death meant to him: It meant the survivors' experience even more than his experience. A combination of genuine suspicion and deep love resulted in a loss of peace for John, after church, at the end of his life.

In clinical pastoral education, we are told that the safest course is to say soft "I" statements. Not preachy "I" statements, but soft ones. Thus, I resisted some asinine definition of tranquility and said, "I have a personal relationship with God and I don't know where it came from, John. It's a place in my belly."

That got his attention. "Yeah, I don't have any place in my belly. What I have is the absence of God in my belly."

Things were deteriorating. We both knew it. Charlotte had gone to get the car and mercifully returned to our stumbling spiritual mumbling and groping.

I am writing now to see whether I can find a way to speak of tranquility. Of course it is calm, the absence of worry. Of course it is peace, the absence of fear about pain or God or meaning. And of course it is time, free from doctors and coughing and oxygen and the details of dying. But tranquility is a presence as well as an absence. John wanted to feel the breath of God in his breath. The soul of God in his soul. The time of God in his time. And he didn't.

Imagine, at his age, in his condition, still hoping that he would.

I think of Isaiah chapter 40 in the Hebrew Scriptures, "Comfort, comfort ye my people, cry to her that her warfare is over." Or the strong words of Psalm 23, "I will fear no evil, for Thou art with me, Thy rod and thy staff, they comfort me." I know John would quip something like, "I am not a sheep."

Tranquility is repeating the old words, though, even if you can't fully believe them. They carry the tranquility in their belly even when we don't carry it in ours. That may be what other people are for—to carry the words we can't believe, to us, when we need them. Then we lean toward each other, stretch toward each other, imitating that leaning and stretching that John was doing toward God. Leaning toward each other is sacred speech; getting it right is too correct.

There are thousands of things we can't say or do right. There are many more incorrect than correct words. Sacred speech understands that and rambles the road, fumbling toward the other in love and incomplete understanding.

9

The Sacredness of Ordinary, Plain Speech

Getting our personal boundaries straight is the prelude to plain speaking. By boundaries I mean our sense of self as we relate to others. Good boundaries mean that we know where we stop and the other starts. We have a self that is protected—and the other can't horn in on our space.

Good boundaries are important to good relationships. Confusion is often the result of confused boundaries. Because security is a gift from God and many of us refuse to show up at the party where the gifts are handed out, we are often confused. We suspect someone is stepping on our toes or think that we have to be "careful" when indeed we might just be being asked to dance. When we don't have good boundaries, we imagine that we have less freedom than we really have. This confusion creates numerous problems; one of them is confused speech.

Sacred speech does not avoid the negative. Holy speech is free to express the negative. It is also free to express the positive. Sacred speech is just plain free, the key reason being that it knows it is protected by personal boundaries. It knows where it stops and where the other starts. "I wish you hadn't said that," a well-bounded person can say with a straight face. Or, "I wish we could just go have coffee" is a plain urge, plainly expressed. "I don't want to talk right now. Can we talk later?" When we say what we really feel, we are often blessed with the holy prosaic. When we say what we don't really feel, we are often cursed with long paragraphs of confused language, body messages that contradict what we are saying, and troubles of multiplying varieties. Even our best friends will interrupt us when we have diarrhea of the mouth. Compare these examples of confusion to those plainly spoken above. "I really wish you hadn't said that but now that you did, I guess we are going to have to stay up all night talking about what you said and how I felt about what you said and how I wish, how I really wish, you hadn't said what you said." "I know you want to go to the movies and you'll probably want to go shopping afterward, but all I really want to do is have some coffee and go home, but I know you won't accept anything like that so I guess we'll have to go to the movies." And, "I really don't have the energy to talk now, but since you are insisting that we do talk now, I guess we will have to do what you want." Note the difference between plain and confused speech. One is short; the other is long. One has a sense of self; the other is full of projections. One says "I" freely; the other says "you" with an edge.

One key to knowing whether we are being clear or not is the matter of length. (One of the most stunning of all scriptures is when God commands the prophet to "make my way plain.") Plain speech is a virtue. We can tell its presence by brevity. How long did it take us to say whatever we said? Did we keep repeating it? How many times did we say it over and over—and what in the world are we justifying? Clarity often finds itself in short sentences. "I don't want to do that just now." "I want this meeting to get to the subject for which it was called." "I fear that some people are doing all the talking and I would like to hear from those who haven't spoken." "I prefer Chinese food." "I think you should have made the last turn." (Can you say that last one in a playful or amusing way?)

Sacred speech is something that is done publicly, intimately, spiritually, electronically, and all the rest—and it also happens in regular, ordinary time. Its art is more precious in the daily than in the cosmic. Good boundaries make ordinary time go smoothly; confused and fuzzy boundaries can keep everyone in a dither for a long time.

To learn how to speak plainly, simply, and beautifully in everyday terms and contexts is not easy, but it is possible. It has most to do with the freedom of internal clarification. What do I want? What are my boundaries? What is enough for me? What does God want of me and from me?

Ninety percent of plain speech is internal discipline. We enter conversations knowing what we want. We leave knowing whether or not we got it. This matter is not selfish but loving. When we know what we want, we also know what we can give. We know how far we will go toward the other—and when we will stop leaning toward the relationship. Clarity is first internal and then expresses itself in sacred speech.

SMALL TALK
AND CASUAL CONVERSATION

One of the things that I really dislike is "small talk," the cocktail party version of relationship. I have taught myself a few tricks so that

I don't have to do much of it. One is to ask a safe question. Instead of asking you where you are from, why don't I ask you where your grandmothers are from? Which one was your favorite? Why? I learned this trick from training in a mental hospital where we did "religious developmental histories" with people who were pretty shut down emotionally and verbally. There is a long process to the history taking, but it can be abbreviated in a number of ways. Most people will tell the story of their distant pasts. The closer to present-day reality we get, the more guarded we are. Thus, questions about your "favorite house ever" or "favorite job ever" can be playful and not intrusive, which is the trick to the holy prosaic in "getting to know you" speech. Again, boundaries matter. We are not "invading" the other so much as coming close with our boundaries touching, but not overlapping, the other's.

Cocktail parties are not the only places where we can be irritated by small talk or by general dither. Think of "small talk" defined; it is what we do when we don't want to do large. I would never say that large talk is what we should do on a bus or in a restroom line. Instead, I would argue that people who know sacred speech love it and covet it in relationships both intimate and ordinary. Learning how to enlarge small talk opportunities is a key to enjoying more of the sacred and less of the profane in our life.

One of the issues that religious leaders face very often is wordiness in meetings. Human beings come together to accomplish goals, and they come together simply to have relationship. Experts on groups argue that successful groups balance two things—task and relationship. Good groups get things done, and they enhance the connections among people. The very trust that emanates from relationship helps people accomplish tasks. Many meetings confuse these two objectives and find people talking endlessly, usually as a veiled form of hope for relationship. Instead of clarifying what we want—as in "I came to this organization to make friends as well as to be of use to someone else"—we circle the matter. We quarrel about the right way to do the task. Or we let a few people dominate the discussion while others are silenced.

Knowing what we want whenever we go into a meeting is very important. Knowing what we want out of a relationship, even our most intimate ones, is very important. When we know the answers to these questions, our speech becomes simple. Our speech comes from our purpose, and that simplifies our language.

Speech That Carries Spirit

When a meeting starts to get boring, or out of control, or dominated, anyone can say, "I need clarification on our purpose here this evening." Or, "I need to know how long we need to attend to this one matter. I have a few other things that seem important that need some airtime too." Or, "I really appreciate the care we have been giving to this one topic and I wish we had all the time in the world to discuss it. Instead, we are limited in our time. When do you think we can move on?"

Sacred speech is spoken by people who feel they have a right to their life. They are not afraid of what they want or embarrassed by it. Instead, they are governed by their own desires for their own life. There is a freedom from Spirit to be spiritual. There is a freedom to be who we are, where we are, when we are there. Good boundaries are actually gifts of the Spirit, who grants us ourselves, freely.

We have to be very careful, though, not to be too spiritual about ordinary speech. Again, we are not trying to make all speech momentous. Instead, we are trying to let simple speech be sacred. One of our members doesn't like "all" the announcements we put at the beginning of the service. She is a senior citizen and enjoys sending me E-mail jokes about her love life. They are often examples of the personals she might put in the paper if she were that sort of lady, which she definitely is not. One joke, for instance, leads with her desire for long-term commitment: "Recent widow who buried fourth husband looking for someone to round out a six-unit plot. Dizziness, fainting, shortness of breath not a problem." These kinds of E-mail jokes can be a very holy exchange between people. They lighten us up. They connect us. They are nonthreatening. They allow us to have "threatening" speech more easily.

I had asked a large group some time ago what sermon topics they wanted. They handed in cards, with topics ranging from plagiarism to the language about God in hymns to why people committed adultery. In a doozy of a letter, my humorous E-mail correspondent asked me to preach about announcements. She said, "They are too long. They lack spirituality. There are too many of them. Even though I hate to be even a nanosecond late to anything, I always come to worship late so I don't have to hear them." Back in the days when people wrote real letters, rather than E-mails, letter writing was a real art. Her letter has art. It argues quite eloquently that our everyday life is bombarded with messages, announcements, pleas that we engage ourselves in activities or that we buy something. We drive on roads with billboards. We listen to radio and televisions with regularized demands on our time and money. My correspondent argues that there needs to be more and more of a degree of separation between *sacer* and *profanus,* the sacred and profane realms of life. Announcements blend the realms. My eloquent friend is opposed to the blend. I humbly disagree.

Don't get me wrong—I appreciate her concerns. As one very good politician put it, "I used to be indecisive about the matter, but now I'm not too sure." The most often raised problem in our church council is the matter of communication. In addition to my friend who wants less communication, there are dozens who want more. You may or may not want it in worship. That is another matter. But we know that we have a hard time getting information about ourselves out. We even have newly supported fears that when we do get information out, people don't listen to it. We are so bombarded by too much information that most of us have a stack somewhere of unread mail, unanswered letters, and unopened magazines. That's where people put our church newsletter, *Good Tidings*—in that big pile. Thus we have experimented recently with longer inserts in the bulletin, shorter inserts in the bulletin, longer *Tidings* or newsletters, or shorter ones. I have a personal pledge that I will make only five announcements per Sunday—and last Sunday I made eight. Why? My experience of the quiet before the Sunday service, especially in June as parish activities wind down, is that five people hand me a small piece of paper on which an absolutely urgent announcement is handwritten. We hunger for plain speech because we are bombarded with embroidered and frivolous speech.

Several members begged me not to announce one more time that worship was now at 10:00 A.M. for the summer; they said they were sick of hearing about it. Others begged me to stop telling about the next Sunday's important happenings—four weeks in a row is enough.

But I have to let you in on a little secret. There will be people showing up for the 10:45 worship week after week, all June, every year.
They will even have heard the announcement. And there will be
people who will declare that nobody told them about next week's
meeting. I promise. Or that nobody explained that we were electing
a new church council. I guarantee it.

At the United Church of Christ Senior Pastors' conference this
year, we did lots of mini surveys of the sixty people gathered. The two
biggest problems—and this is scary—in our larger churches are
length of announcements and parking. Trivial? I don't think so. Small
enough matters, yes, but not trivial. People cannot accept the invitation to God if they don't hear it, and people cannot worship God if
they can't park their car. Still, I understand the delicious complexity
of the matter: The profane loves to edge out the sacred.

In sacred speech, we elevate the profane. We do not lower the
sacred. We communicate from and to God while talking to each
other. For some people—and these are my favorite kinds of people—
anything less than a personal invitation doesn't count. Many people
want narrowcast, not broadcast. If something is broadcast, we close
our ears. We think we are special enough for personal invitations.
And, by the grace of God, so we are. We are the kind of people who
have heard the call of the holy in our lives and we know its crystal
ping. We know the good wine from the bad, the good music from the
bad, and the good literature from the bad. We cringe in Macy's at holiday time, when we stand over the underwear counter and hear some
tinny version of *Silent Night* moving in on our ears. We may or may not
be communications experts, but we know when we are being talked at
and we know when we are being talked to. Announcements, unfortunately, talk at people. They are bread thrown at the water to see who is

hungry. They are a necessary evil. One person may come to that writing workshop we announced for next weekend and find that he or she can write. Is that worth all the noise pollution, flyers, and paper we have wasted on it? I think so. I also think there is a better way to bring a sense of personal invitation into our lives. It is grounded in the holiness of ordinary speech.

Consider Jesus' words on the ordinary lily as an example. "Consider the lilies of the field how they neither sow nor reap but how God, nevertheless, takes care of them. I tell you even Solomon, in all his glory, was not arrayed as one of these." This text opens up two holy ideas to us—and they matter more than all the rest. One is a sense of expectation. We can expect to be taken care of. We don't need to fear that we will not be taken care of. We don't need to fear bad things.

The other idea is more deeply embedded in the first idea. It is a sense of invitation that joins the sense of expectation. We are invited to consider ourselves as beautiful as a lily in the field. We are invited to consider our basic goodness—not our capacity to perform or work, be useful or toil admirably, attend lots of workshops or none. We are invited to consider—and to expect—that we are as good as the lilies in the field and as good as Solomon in all his glory. Just as

> Fog, confusion, and verbosity are the opposites of sacred speech. Sacred speech is simple and concise. If we are talking in long, circular paragraphs or repeating ourselves incessantly, we are not speaking in a sacred way. Something is bothering us. We are not well bounded—and we are reaching for others in a way that probably won't find them. We are trying to please and desperate to connect rather than trying to be ourselves—the only genuine way to connect in the first place. Listen for the short and simple. It is the gateway to the holy.

we are. This is the announcement at the heart of my faith as a Christian. That we are saved by grace, not by works. That we are in the eyes of our Creator beautiful.

When we give the other announcements at the beginning of the service, we invite each other to join this fundamental announcement in a thousand shapes. We say to each other that we expect goodness and will be meeting at 7:30 P.M. on Tuesday to enjoy it.

Sacred speech refuses to hit people over the head with the holy. Instead, it invites and draws out. Sacred speech has to be prosaic and ordinary because it must have steps that help people "climb" to God. Plain speech is not just a ladder to God or even short, well-bounded sentences purely and freely spoken. Plain speech also packages some of the most attractive invitations in very small invitational sentences.

We know, for example, that most clergy became clergy because someone invited them. Someone said, "You may have the gift of holy vocation. Have you ever thought about going to seminary?" More simply, in ordinary life, "I am so glad you are part of our temple, church, organization, Rotary, women's club, whatever. I'd love to get to know you better. Are you free for coffee?"

Marlo Thomas's book *The Right Words at the Right Time* emphasizes the capacity of invitation.[1] We don't talk at length so much as in a focused way when we find ourselves asking the right question at the right time. I always get nervous at this point in discussing the holiness of the act of invitation. Sometimes we make "announcements" because we are so afraid to actually invite someone to something. We are so afraid that he or she will say no or that we will be rejected. Many people hate to ask others for money precisely because it feels so invasive. What I know about some of us is that we need our space; we need to be in conversations where we are assured that we are safe. So when I have to ask for money, I try to use sacred speech: "Would you mind if I asked you a personal question? I simply love this organization and have found such joy here. I hope you have too—and that you will think about increasing your contribution here this year. If I have offended you, please forgive me. I know we are all in different places. . . ."

In my kind of Protestant tradition, we often need to be sprinkled—not dunked—with a message. We need a chance to dip our toes in the joy; we don't like to jump in the way kids leap into a pool, with a lot of razzmatazz and splashing. You can see my problem, though. Jesus says this astonishing thing about us—that we are as good as the lilies in the field, that God is not going to let any wind or rain destroy our flowering. We are as rich as Solomon, too. Perhaps you are wondering about what Solomon would do with all your credit card debt, or you are wound up so tight that you fear your bud will never flower but instead stay coiled and tense and undeveloped. Or you have just been too polluted by too much information that turned out not to be true, like the contractor who said he would show up on Friday and never did. These disparities between spiritual reality—God's announcement, invitation, and expectation—and our lived experience are the core of the problem. That's why we have programs and "steps" to help people come to God. In sacred speech, we don't drive people into the joy with vigor; we invite them to the joy with grace. We keep our questions "open" and don't box each other in. We risk the right word for the right time—and when we are wrong, we are well bounded enough to apologize and move on and give the other person space.

SPEAKING OF ORDINARY,
BUT DELICATE, MATTERS

Speech That Carries Spirit

At a conference recently, I met a poet I really liked who clearly had some kind of shaking disease. I assumed it was Parkinson's. Whenever he read his work or talked at the dinner table, he began to shake fairly vigorously. I was torn about whether to ask him about his tremor. Not asking meant I didn't want to know him. Asking meant I could invade him. Thus, I waited until the third and final night of the conference and said, "Do you mind if I ask you why you shake?" "No," he said. "I have Parkinson's." I was able to say that I was sorry and to find out how long he had had it and what his prognosis was. He later said to me that it bothered him when people didn't ask; he felt as if they didn't care about him or his reality.

When it comes to delicate matters, we can go right or wrong. Well-bounded people care enough about the prosaic to ask the questions and to risk mistakes. There is a commercial from a wine maker that says it well. The wine maker's journal reads for Tuesday, "Have removed more leaves today to allow just a fraction more light to reach the grapes. This will transform the fruit's intensity, adding character and richness to the wine." Sacred speech opens people up to one another. It brings them to the right proximity and throws the light of the holy on what is happening between them.

Announcements also "en-lighten." Next week's writing program might allow just a fraction more light to touch someone's developing soul. The youth trip to Little Haiti could do the same. The spirituality of announcements is in their invitational quality; they are an invitation to God's feast and God's joy, God's security and God's hope. If they are not, may they be abolished. Sacred speech can make even announcements holy.

Of course, some people don't need careful invitations to the joy and juice of life. Some are ready to jump into the pool with all their clothes on right now. Announcements and graded curricula of the Spirit are not for everybody. There is a truth in spirited living that can engage us; that mountain of credit card debt has nothing to do with who we really are. The way you are shut down, coiled up, angered, and endangered as a member of the human race—that too has nothing to do with who God made you to be. Open up! Just open up. We can open with or without the invitation. And we can open, with or without a sense of the other. Well-bounded people have space in which to move from bud to flower. That is the kind of freedom we enjoy. From that freedom we speak.

There is nothing easy about getting our sacred speech right. We can err by getting too close or staying too distant. We can "flower" and get pollen all over someone else and not even know we are doing it! We can be too intimate or not intimate enough. Sacred speech is difficult. But we speak it in the name of the opening of the rosebud or lily, in the name of the slowly opening wing of a bird that is ready to fly. One African-American preacher put it like this: "You can bang the cymbal too soon. You can bang the cymbal too late. But what is important is that you do bang the cymbal." That sums up the issue with sacred speech, the kind that opens and invites, the kind that brims with expectation about life's goodness. It's not easy, but it is important to bang the cymbal.

There may be just one more possibility for people who want to make the ordinary holy through their words. It could be that what the lily actually does in the field is simply to wait, with expectation for the care that God provides. When waiting, we too become engaged with God, and then we fill up and spill over. We are different from the group that needs to be repeatedly invited, carefully opened so as not to destroy the fragility of the bud or flower. We are not just "fast" or "slow" spiritually. There is another group. We expect an invitation—but we haven't heard it yet. In V. S. Naipaul's book *Half a Life,* the author writes that all his life he had been waiting. "All that he [Naipaul] had now was an idea—and it was like a belief in magic—that one day something would happen, an illumination would come to him, and he would be taken by a set of events to the place he would go. What he had to do was to hold himself in readiness, to recognize the moment."[2] I suspect that many, many people have found themselves waiting for something to happen, something magical or momentous or prodigious that, once recognized, would change everything. For people who have considered the lilies, we know that something momentous has already happened: The sacred is real to us in ordinary ways, at meetings, at cocktail parties, on buses, and on trains. We have very little fear and lots and lots of joy. We know what we want, which is to be in relationship with God and with each other. We are clear, not fuzzy, about that. Thus, engagement is automatic. We expect it. And we invite others as well. Engagement, properly bounded, results in a fairly constant flow of invitational, ordinary speech. We don't say much, but what we do say matters to many.

10

The Importance
of Silence

We often know the value of words when they are absent. We often
know them in what musicians call the caesura, or rest between notes.
Silence punctuates the sacred nature of words. It can be as much a
blessing as the holy prosaic. Henry David Thoreau speaks of the
quiet that is a form of deep attention. He describes his mornings as
full of this holy quiet. He would choose to sit outside his door and
not get to "work" until he was ready to move from the deepest of
quiets into a little bit of noise. Very few of us know what quiet is anymore. Stop and listen right now. What do you hear? Cars humming,
perhaps a bird or two, the radio. Rarely do we know moments of
pure quiet in the modern world. As we complete our attention on
sacred speech, it is important to recognize how much quiet con-
tributes to it.

Speech That Carries Spirit

A woman has been multitasking all day long. She has picked up the kids, picked up the house, folded the laundry, talked on the phone to her mother and sister, worked an eight-hour day, and fought traffic on the way home. She is making more lists of how to spend the evening profitably when she realizes that, by some mistake, she is early for her meeting. There is a park next door to the meeting place and she finds herself driving there. She parks her car in front of the lake in the park, noting just how many working vans are there—the phone company, the tree company, and the roofing company. She wonders what all these workers are doing here, just sitting. That's when she realizes that she hasn't "just sat" for weeks, maybe months. She pushes her seat into a reclining position and daydreams a bit. It might be a nap, it might be a meditation, and it might be both. That night at the meeting, she is as articulate and useful as she has ever been. The same focus helps her get the kids to sleep; she is actually interested in them as opposed to trying to hurry them off to bed. Why? She has been quiet long enough to speak.

This kind of quiet is richly valued by those who can stand it. Many cannot; many will fill up any empty space with Muzak or talk or television. They are missing something. They are missing what Thoreau calls the "extra," or abundance of quietness. Not all quiet is good. Some quiet is the quiet of fear, what Dr. Martin Luther King Jr. called the appalling silence of the good people. That silence is not sacred. The sacred comes when fear is quieted and something like peace prevails. In Thoreau's mornings, there was a holy quiet. If he had been avoiding important conversation or connection rather than enjoying nature, there would have been nothing holy about his quiet.

In the uncanny way some of us have of being struck dumb when we think someone else is in charge of our lives and our tongues rather than us, there is nothing holy. Consider the prophecy in Isaiah 53:7: "He was oppressed, and he was afflicted, yet he did not open his mouth; like a lamb that is led to the slaughter, and like a sheep that before its shearers is silent, so he did not open his mouth." There are times we must speak, when quiet is a cage and a hiding place. There are also times when quiet and silence are blessed and when they "feed" sacred speech.

Learning to distinguish between positive forms of silence and negative ones is a task of sacred speech. There may be times when even the "silence of the good people" is necessary. Some moments are better than others for speech. I often think that when something really bad happens, the best thing to do is raise the issue an hour later or the next morning.

An associate of mine managed to violate our funeral payment policy. Pastors, organists, and soloists receive a set fee for a non-member funeral in our church. That fee is a generous hundred dollars. If the bereaved family gives more than that amount of money to the church, the money goes into the general fund. My associate didn't understand the policy, and so when a particularly generous person gave a thousand-dollar contribution, the associate distributed the money three ways among himself, the organist, and the soloist. The other organists and soloists were very upset; they worked the same amount of time, in other funerals, for a very different amount of money. Instead of laying into him right after the service, I waited until the next day and spoke softly about the policy and its violation. The restraint proved fruitful: The policy was observed and the money was redistributed. No one was hurt, and no one was embarrassed or required to react in the afterglow of a meaningful funeral experience. If restraint can help in such a small situation, imagine its potential in a larger matter.

There are also many positive ways to communicate with each other without words. I think of the way some people just glow when they are around their beloved—their child or their dog or their lover. To glow means to let light from within out. Words are often unnecessary and can get in the way of the glow. We don't need words all the time. I remember seeing a very interesting sculpture that was lit from above. It was just two tall cylinders meant to evoke a human form, made exactly in the artist's own body dimensions of height and weight. Lit from above, though, the columns seemed almost alive. We know people who bear themselves this way; they seem lit from the inside. They glow. In that glowing, there is tremendously sacred communication, toward others and toward oneself. Perhaps even Spirit is pleased.

> There are positive and negative forms of silence. In the positive, we attend deeply to Spirit; in the negative, we are fumbling and don't know why. There is nothing wrong with not knowing or being quiet in the face of the unknowable. We might even call it awe. Those who find their way to sacred speech often find their way by treasuring the silence, both the positive and the negative kinds.

There may be as many forms of silence as Inuits have words for snow. There is also the silence and quiet of being struck dumb. One day I looked down at my hand and the diamond in my ring was gone. The stone had slipped away, right out of the ring's setting, and all that was left was metal. Promised to my daughter, my grandmother's ring was now close to worthless. In defiance and disbelief, I wore it for days . . . just that way. No one noticed. I couldn't stop looking at the empty hole where the diamond had been. No one else bothered. I finally got to the place where I could tell my husband and daughter that the diamond was gone. I had been flabbergasted into silence.

There is also the silence of being comfortable with another. Although some couples see their wedding or commitment ceremony as the moment when everything from their bank accounts to their taste in food must merge, D. H. Lawrence writes about two people in a relationship being like two stars who rotate around each other, attracted by each other's energy but not dependent on each other. On a train or a plane, we often see couples who simply sit together, quietly, in peaceful companionship. There is something very sacred to their nonverbal speech.

There are sacred silences and profane silences. I think of old people sitting alone in apartments playing solitaire. They are simply being. A holy silence is one that is kept toward God. When we don't "have" to say anything, we are often in deep communion with our Maker, solitaire or no solitaire. We simply accept the joy of being.

There is the silence that comes when there is nothing more to say. Unlike Dr. Seuss, who persevered through twenty-seven rejections before his first book was finally published, we sometimes grow silent and stop "submitting" our prose because we just don't want to be hurt or rejected anymore. We want to leave well enough alone. We have nothing more to say. We are plumb out of the courage to try, speak, engage, or carry on. That silence can be holy, too—especially when Spirit joins us in our passive and hopeful waiting.

GIVING SPEECH A SABBATH

Sometimes we retreat to sacred silence on purpose. We want to take a moratorium on things. We give a Sabbath break to our speech. People go on three-day meditations and "keep silence." Or they lie in bed for a long time in the morning, just thinking. On such occasions, we realize just how overwhelmed we are by the too-muchness of it all.

Sometimes our silence comes because we just don't know what to say. We are hung up on politically correct language—such as the "right" way to sing the doxology—and rather than side with either group in our parish, we just shut our mouths. We don't speak. We may want to sing "Creator, Christ, and Holy Ghost" at the end of the doxology, or we may want to sing "Father, Son, and Holy Ghost," or we may not want to sing any such thing, but no matter what, we offend someone. Thus, we find ourselves silent in confusion and fear.

The newsletter of the Center for Progressive Christianity defends the use of the word *Lord* to those Christians who would no longer use it. Some are offended by the masculine in the word; others think it implies the subjugation of subjects. The English word *Lord* comes from *hlaford,* a contraction of "loaf" and "warden." The Lord is understood in that context as the keeper of the bread. The Lord protected the market in which wheat was grown and sold. Multifaith, post-denominational, and post-liturgical people are uncomfortable with established religions. They fear them. We may be in a pregnant pause in this period of liturgical silence and indecision. That kind of silence may be the forerunner of a new Vatican III, or we may just find ourselves nudged toward new speech in ways we can't yet begin to imagine. I have been in Christian congregations that war over whether to say the ancient formula "May the Lord be with you," and I have been in congregations that prefer to stay quiet on matters like these until the new words come. I have also been in congregations that go to premature war over correct liturgical speech. Some of the silence is sacred; other instances of it are cowardly. We need good, long quiet to know which is which—and when to hold our tongue and when to use it.

Ancient texts actually have a lot to say about how God makes us mute. They suggest that, in fact, it is God who mutes us. Surely there is a silence in which God intervenes against talkativeness on behalf of the silence. In the Torah, in Exodus 4:11, we are told, "Then the lord said to him, 'Who gives speech to mortals? Who makes them mute or deaf, seeing or blind? Is it not I?'"

While speech is understood as bold and necessary, silence is understood as an option. It is a lesser option, but an option nonetheless. We are, according to Proverbs 31:8, to "speak out for those who cannot speak, for the rights of all the destitute." The promise of glad speech is important to hear: "Then the lame shall leap like a deer, and the tongue of the speechless sing for joy. For waters shall break forth in the wilderness, and streams in the desert" (Isaiah 35:6). We are awakened into speech and numbed and dumbed into silence, as in the curse of Ezekiel 3:26: "And I will make your tongue cling to the roof of your mouth, so that you shall be speechless and unable to reprove them; for they are a rebellious house." The contrasts between a cursed silence and a blessed speech occur throughout the ancient text. In Ezekiel 24:27, we hear a report of a good day: "On that day your mouth shall be opened to the one who has escaped, and you shall speak and no longer be silent. So you shall be a sign to them; and they shall know that I am the Lord."

The many different kinds of silence, while blessed, do not compete with the excellence of sacred speech. Being struck "dumb" is not a blessing. That condition is not sacred silence or restraint. It is a form of punishment and widely considered a disability.

One more form of silence is important. It is the silence of awe before God. Many biblical figures are struck dumb in the presence of God. Consider the Torah again, from Deuteronomy 10:15: "While he was speaking these words to me, I turned my face toward the ground, and was speechless." Additionally, the Christian Gospels are full of examples of those who have been mute and are liberated into speech by a healing miracle. The following are my own favorites for devotional meditation.

> Matthew 9:32 After they had gone away, a demoniac who was mute was brought to him.

> Matthew 9:33 And when the demon had been cast out, the one who had been mute spoke and the crowds were amazed and said, "Never has anything like this been seen in Israel."

> Matthew 12:22 Then they brought to him a demoniac who was blind and mute; and he cured him, so that the one who had been mute could speak and see.

> Matthew 15:30 Great crowds came to him, bringing with them the lame, the maimed, the blind, the mute, and many others. They put them at his feet, and he cured them.

> Matthew 15:31 The crowd was amazed when they saw the mute speaking, the maimed whole, the lame walking, and the blind seeing. And they praised the God of Israel.

> Mark 7:37 They were astounded beyond measure, saying, "He has done everything well; he even makes the deaf to hear and the mute to speak."

Mark 9:17 Someone from the crowd answered him, "Teacher, I brought you my son; he has a spirit that makes him unable to speak."

Mark 9:25 When Jesus saw that a crowd came running together, he rebuked the unclean spirit, saying to it, "You spirit that keeps this boy from speaking and hearing, I command you, come out of him, and never enter him again!"

Luke 1:20 "But now, because you did not believe my words, which will be fulfilled in their time, you will become mute, unable to speak, until the day these things occur."

Luke 11:14 Now he was casting out a demon that was mute; when the demon had gone out, the one who had been mute spoke, and the crowds were amazed.

Awe can strike us dumb and awe can be the sight of a miracle. We can find our way from awe to deeper silence or to deeper speech. The presence of Spirit makes the difference.

Those of us trained in the seminary know that we are often advised not to say anything. The training goes like this: If a person tells you something that frightens you or horrifies you, simply mumble, "Hmm" or answer, "Yes, I understand." If a person says that her father raped her, we are not to be startled. If he says that his mother was an incest victim and so is he, we are to be very quiet. The more quiet we can have in the receipt of the difficult news, the better. That means the person can keep talking without having to take care of us. Eventually, we can express our dismay and our lament. But when a person first opens up, we are not to show our fear of the news. There is also a silence that receives and doesn't give back or speak back until the gift of the other is fully received.

I have violated this training at my own peril. Once a clergyperson whom I was supervising in a parish called late at night to say that he had cursed out his board of deacons in a meeting earlier that night. Worse, he had used the "F-word" to the chairperson. Instead of restraint or a holy silence, I said, *"You did what?"* My overreaction only condemned him. More grace was needed. The grace could have come by a respectful silence.

Again, knowing when to speak and when to stay quiet is a delicate and exquisite dilemma. When we are not really sure what to do, it is almost always better to stay quiet. Speech sometimes can't be undone, but quiet can be interrupted. Ministers can give this kind of advice because most of us have made so many really interesting mistakes! By "minister" I mean any person who lives in the dangerous, exhilarating, life-giving borderlands of human existence, where the everyday experience of life opens up to reveal glimpses of the holy—and not only lives there but also comes to the aid of others who are living there. I owe this wonderful definition to L. William Countryman, who used it in his essay "Living on the Border of the Holy."

Whether we are ordained or not, ministers can make good mistakes when faced with the great variety of numbness and silence that exists. Knowing whether to speak or not to speak takes a kind of wisdom that is rarely known or seen.

Sacred speech can take us to hard places—in lament and judgment. Forgiveness can carry us forward to the softer places where sacred speech also helps. There we pray and praise and love, as humbly as possible. Silence puts margin on the page of speech—and we find the love that lives beyond fear.

Notes

CHAPTER 1: TO BE HUMBLE

1. Kofi Annan, in a letter to alumni of Macalester College, published in *Mac Wire* (September 2001).

CHAPTER 2: TO FORGIVE

1. Robert Folger, "Trust and Controversy," *Chronicle of Higher Education* (April 12, 2002), B13.
2. Cynthia Polansky, *Far Above Rubies* (n.p.: Booklocker.com, 2001).

CHAPTER 3: TO PRAISE

1. Doris Sommer, "Speaking in Tongues," *Chronicle of Higher Education* (June 7, 2002): B4.
2. Lewis Thomas, *The Medusa and the Snail* (New York: Viking, 1979), 28.
3. George Herbert, "Come, My Way, My Truth, My Life," in *New Century Hymnal* (Cleveland: Pilgrim Press, 1997), hymn no. 331.

CHAPTER 6: TO LAMENT

1. Brian Wren, "Telling Truth through Tearful Songs," *Journal for Preachers* (Columbia Theological Seminary, forthcoming, 2003).
2. Shirley Erena Murray, "God Weeps," (Carol Stream, Ill.: Hope Publishing Co., 1996).

CHAPTER 7: TO LOVE

1. Quoted in Paul Murray, "The Grand Aquinas," *Spirituality* 7, no. 39 (Nov.–Dec. 2001): 362ff.

CHAPTER 8: BEYOND THE POLITICALLY CORRECT

1. Vivian Paley, *You Can't Say You Can't Play* (Cambridge: Harvard Univ. Press, 1993).
2. Prayer by Reinhold Niebuhr, which is often reprinted in church bulletins and newsletters.

CHAPTER 9: THE SACREDNESS OF ORDINARY, PLAIN SPEECH

1. Marlo Thomas, ed., *The Right Words at the Right Time* (New York: Atria Books, 2002).
2. V. S. Naipaul, *Half a Life* (New York: Knopf, 2001), 254.

Sacred Speech: A Practical Guide for Keeping Spirit in Your Speech

Discussion Guide

CHAPTER 1: TO BE HUMBLE

1. Humility is reaching toward the other, even when the other is being unfair. How difficult is it to be humble in speech?

2. What are some ways to avoid self-justifying?

3. Think of an instance where you have seen the expression of humility in someone's speech or behavior. What reaction did you have?

4. How can we let go of our very human need to be right all of the time in our speech? What do we gain from being right? What do we lose?

CHAPTER 2: TO FORGIVE

1. Sacred speech gets to the words of forgiveness as quickly as it can after something bad happens. How can we move toward forgiving someone who has hurt us? What is a good "first step"? A good "second step"?

2. When we are angry or hurt or confused, we can use the simple godly tool of asking a question: "Could you tell me more?" Are there occasions in your conversations when this response would create more understanding and less hurt?

CHAPTER 3: TO PRAISE

1. Praising the world as it is while praising the world for what it will yet be requires faith in God's goodness. How could this kind of praise and hope infuse more Spirit in your speech?

2. What is your favorite "language" of praise? Do you sing? Dance? Preach?

CHAPTER 4: TO PRAY

1. The sacred words of prayer don't "make" God appear; they take us to the God who is already there. How does prayer reach out to Spirit? Describe a time when you were surprised to realize that God was there all along, though you hadn't called.

2. What are the risks we take in praying openly, in public? How are these risks holy?

3. What special considerations surround interfaith or multifaith prayer? What are the special challenges of sacred speech in interfaith or multifaith situations?

CHAPTER 5: TO JUDGE

1. Sacred speech learns to speak the truth in love. How can judgment be sacred speech? What are some of the words that you've found to be healing and holy?

2. Think of an instance where trouble happened and people said, "Why didn't anybody say anything sooner?" How could taking the risk of sacred speech have changed the outcome?

CHAPTER 6: TO LAMENT

1. When we lament, we trust God enough to show how forsaken or distressed we feel and we show our desire for God's help. How can we let Spirit help us to express the pain that feels inexpressible?

2. How can sacred speech liberate us to heal?

3. Lament can be used sacredly in personal, spiritual, and political areas of life. What can be achieved through specifically directed laments and their necessary hope for reconciliation?

CHAPTER 7: TO LOVE

1. Love allows us to use sacred speech to tell each other who we really are, to let another person see us as we see ourselves. In what ways do you use sacred speech in your family? In your friendships?

2. Is it possible/practical/proper to practice the sacred speech of love at work? How?

3. How can we express our love as "unconditional"? How can we show it in our speech?

CHAPTER 8: BEYOND THE POLITICALLY CORRECT

1. What is the difference between being correct and being truthful?

2. Can you remember instances where someone's insistence on being "politically correct" resulted in shutting down all conversation?

3. Reaching toward others is a way of moving beyond politically correct speech to sacred speech. How do you show other people that you are open, approachable?

CHAPTER 9: THE SACREDNESS OF ORDINARY, PLAIN SPEECH

1. Inner clarity leads to sacred speech. Exercise: To learn how to speak plainly, ask yourself these questions about a particular issue:

   • What do I want?

   • Where are my boundaries?

   • What is enough for me?

   • What does God want of me and from me?

   Rephrase your answers into simple, ordinary statements—into sacred speech.

CHAPTER 10: THE IMPORTANCE OF SILENCE

1. Silence can be sacred in itself. When have you found solace in being quiet? What's the difference in the quality of holy silence when you are alone and when you are in the company of others?

2. Do you ever use silence to prepare yourself for sacred speech?

3. Knowing whether to speak or not to speak takes wisdom. What signals you to keep sacred silence in a particular situation?

About the Author

Rev. Donna Schaper is widely recognized as one of the most out-standing communicators in her generation of Protestant clergy. A minister of the United Church of Christ, she is author of numerous books, including *Alone but Not Lonely: A Spirituality of Solitude; Sabbath Sense;* and *Labyrinths from the Outside In: Walking to Spiritual Insight—a Beginner's Guide* (SkyLight Paths).

About SKYLIGHT PATHS Publishing

SkyLight Paths Publishing is creating a place where people of different spiritual traditions come together for challenge and inspiration, a place where we can help each other understand the mystery that lies at the heart of our existence.

Through spirituality, our religious beliefs are increasingly becoming a part of our lives—rather than *apart* from our lives. While many of us may be more interested than ever in spiritual growth, we may be less firmly planted in traditional religion. Yet, we do want to deepen our relationship to the sacred, to learn from our own as well as from other faith traditions, and to practice in new ways.

SkyLight Paths sees both believers and seekers as a community that increasingly transcends traditional boundaries of religion and denomination—people wanting to learn from each other, *walking together, finding the way.*

We at SkyLight Paths take great care to produce beautiful books that present meaningful spiritual content in a form that reflects the art of making high quality books. Therefore, we want to acknowledge those who contributed to the production of this book.

PRODUCTION
Sara Dismukes, Tim Holtz,
Martha McKinney & Bridgett Taylor

EDITORIAL
Rebecca Castellano, Amanda Dupuis, Polly Short Mahoney,
Lauren Seidman, Maura D. Shaw & Emily Wichland

COVER DESIGN
Bridgett Taylor

TEXT DESIGN
Susan Ramundo, SR Desktop Services, Ridge, New York

PRINTING & BINDING
Transcontinental Printing, Peterborough, Ontario

Other Interesting Books—Spirituality

Lighting the Lamp of Wisdom: *A Week Inside a Yoga Ashram*
by *John Ittner;* Foreword by *Dr. David Frawley*

This insider's guide to Hindu spiritual life takes you into a typical week of retreat inside a yoga ashram to demystify the experience and show you what to expect from your own visit. Includes a discussion of worship services, meditation and yoga classes, chanting and music, work practice, and more.

6 x 9, 192 pp, b/w photographs, Quality PB, ISBN 1-893361-52-7 **$15.95**;
HC, ISBN 1-893361-37-3 **$24.95**

Waking Up: *A Week Inside a Zen Monastery*
by *Jack Maguire;* Foreword by *John Daido Loori, Roshi*

An essential guide to what it's like to spend a week inside a Zen Buddhist monastery.
6 x 9, 224 pp, b/w photographs, HC, ISBN 1-893361-13-6 **$21.95**

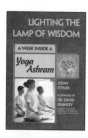   

Making a Heart for God: *A Week Inside a Catholic Monastery*
by *Dianne Aprile;* Foreword by *Brother Patrick Hart,* OCSO

This essential guide to experiencing life in a Catholic monastery takes you to the Abbey of Gethsemani—the Trappist monastery in Kentucky that was home to author Thomas Merton— to explore the details. "More balanced and informative than the popular *The Cloister Walk* by Kathleen Norris." —*Choice: Current Reviews for Academic Libraries*

6 x 9, 224 pp, b/w photographs, Quality PB, ISBN 1-893361-49-7 **$16.95**;
HC, ISBN 1-893361-14-4 **$21.95**

Come and Sit: *A Week Inside Meditation Centers*
by *Marcia Z. Nelson;* Foreword by *Wayne Teasdale*

The insider's guide to meditation in a variety of different spiritual traditions. Traveling through Buddhist, Hindu, Christian, Jewish, and Sufi traditions, this essential guide takes you to different meditation centers to meet the teachers and students and learn about the practices, demystifying the meditation experience.

6 x 9, 224 pp, b/w photographs, Quality PB, ISBN 1-893361-35-7 **$16.95**

Or phone, fax, mail or e-mail to: SKYLIGHT PATHS Publishing
Sunset Farm Offices, Route 4 • P.O. Box 237 • Woodstock, Vermont 05091
Tel: (802) 457-4000 • Fax: (802) 457-4004 • www.skylightpaths.com
Credit card orders: (800) 962-4544 (8:30AM–5:30PM ET Monday–Friday)
Generous discounts on quantity orders. SATISFACTION GUARANTEED. Prices subject to change.

Spirituality

The Art of Public Prayer, 2nd Ed.: *Not for Clergy Only*
by *Lawrence A. Hoffman*

The classic resource for people looking to change worship patterns that stand in the way of everyday spirituality. Empowers us to claim public prayer as our own and to revitalize worship in congregations of all backgrounds. Written for both laypeople and clergy.
6 x 9, 288 pp, Quality PB, ISBN 1-893361-06-3 **$17.95**

Spiritual Manifestos: *Visions for Renewed Religious Life in America from Young Spiritual Leaders of Many Faiths*
Edited by *Niles Elliot Goldstein*; Preface by *Martin E. Marty*

Discover the reasons why so many people have kept organized religion at arm's length.

Here, ten young spiritual leaders, most in their mid-thirties, representing the spectrum of religious traditions—Protestant, Catholic, Jewish, Buddhist, Unitarian Universalist—present the innovative ways they are transforming our spiritual communities and our lives. "These ten articulate young spiritual leaders engender hope for the vitality of 21st-century religion."
—Forrest Church, Minister of All Souls Church in New York City
6 x 9, 256 pp, HC, ISBN 1-893361-09-8 **$21.95**

  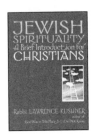 

Jewish Spirituality: *A Brief Introduction for Christians*
by *Lawrence Kushner*

Lawrence Kushner, whose award-winning books have brought Jewish spirituality to life for countless readers of all faiths and backgrounds, tailors his unique style to address Christians' questions, revealing the essence of Judaism in a way that people whose own tradition traces its roots to Judaism can understand and enjoy.
5½ x 8½, 112 pp, Quality PB, ISBN 1-58023-150-0 **$12.95**

The Geography of Faith
Underground Conversations on Religious, Political and Social Change
by *Daniel Berrigan* and *Robert Coles*; Updated introduction and afterword by the authors

A classic of faith-based activism—updated for a new generation.

Listen in on the conversations between these two great teachers—one a renegade priest wanted by the FBI for his protests against the Vietnam war, the other a future Pulitzer Prize-winning journalist—as they struggle with what it means to put your faith to the test. Discover how their story of challenging the status quo during a time of great political, religious, and social change is just as applicable to our lives today. 6 x 9, 224 pp, Quality PB, ISBN 1-893361-40-3 **$16.95**

Spiritual Biography

The Life of Evelyn Underhill
An Intimate Portrait of the Groundbreaking Author of Mysticism
by *Margaret Cropper*; Foreword by *Dana Greene*

Evelyn Underhill was a passionate writer and teacher who wrote elegantly on mysticism, worship, and devotional life. This is the story of how she made her way toward spiritual maturity, from her early days of agnosticism to the years when her influence was felt throughout the world. 6 x 9, 288 pp, 5 b/w photos, Quality PB, ISBN 1-893361-70-5 **$18.95**

Zen Effects: *The Life of Alan Watts*
by *Monica Furlong*

The first and only full-length biography of one of the most charismatic spiritual leaders of the twentieth century—now back in print!

Through his widely popular books and lectures, Alan Watts (1915–1973) did more to introduce Eastern philosophy and religion to Western minds than any figure before or since. Here is the only biography of this charismatic figure, who served as Zen teacher, Anglican priest, lecturer, academic, entertainer, a leader of the San Francisco renaissance, and author of more than 30 books, including *The Way of Zen, Psychotherapy East and West* and *The Spirit of Zen.*
6 x 9, 264 pp, Quality PB, ISBN 1-893361-32-2 **$16.95**

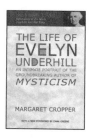   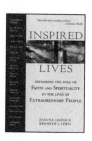

Simone Weil: *A Modern Pilgrimage*
by *Robert Coles*

The extraordinary life of the spiritual philosopher who's been called both saint and madwoman.

The French writer and philosopher Simone Weil (1906–1943) devoted her life to a search for God—while avoiding membership in organized religion. Robert Coles' intriguing study of Weil details her short, eventful life, and is an insightful portrait of the beloved and controversial thinker whose life and writings influenced many (from T. S. Eliot to Adrienne Rich to Albert Camus), and continue to inspire seekers everywhere. 6 x 9, 208 pp, Quality PB, ISBN 1-893361-34-9 **$16.95**

Inspired Lives: *Exploring the Role of Faith and Spirituality in the Lives of Extraordinary People*
by *Joanna Laufer* and *Kenneth S. Lewis*

Contributors include *Ang Lee, Wynton Marsalis, Kathleen Norris, Hakeem Olajuwon, Christopher Parkening, Madeleine L'Engle, Doc Watson,* and many more

In this moving book, soul-searching conversations unearth the importance of spirituality and personal faith for more than forty artists and innovators who have made a real difference in our world through their work. 6 x 9, 256 pp, Quality PB, ISBN 1-893361-33-0 **$16.95**

Spiritual Practice

Women Pray
Voices through the Ages, from Many Faiths, Cultures, and Traditions
Edited and with introductions by *Monica Furlong*

Many ways—new and old—to communicate with the Divine.

This beautiful gift book celebrates the rich variety of ways women around the world have called out to the Divine—with words of joy, praise, gratitude, wonder, petition, longing, and even anger—from the ancient world up to our own time. Prayers from women of nearly every religious or spiritual background give us an eloquent expression of what it means to communicate with God. 5 x7¼,256 pp, Deluxe HC with ribbon marker, ISBN 1-893361-25-X **$19.95**

Praying with Our Hands: *Twenty-One Practices of Embodied Prayer from the World's Spiritual Traditions*
by *Jon M. Sweeney*; Photographs by *Jennifer J. Wilson*;
Foreword by *Mother Tessa Bielecki*; Afterword by *Taitetsu Unno, Ph.D.*

A spiritual guidebook for bringing prayer into our bodies.

This inspiring book of reflections and accompanying photographs shows us twenty-one simple ways of using our hands to speak to God, to enrich our devotion and ritual. All express the various approaches of the world's religious traditions to bringing the body into worship. Spiritual traditions represented include Anglican, Sufi, Zen, Roman Catholic, Yoga, Shaker, Hindu, Jewish, Pentecostal, Eastern Orthodox, and many others.
8 x 8, 96 pp, 22 duotone photographs, Quality PB, ISBN 1-893361-16-0 **$16.95**

   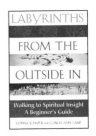

The Sacred Art of Listening
Forty Reflections for Cultivating a Spiritual Practice
by *Kay Lindahl*; Illustrations by *Amy Schnapper*

More than ever before, we need to embrace the skills and practice of listening. You will learn to: Speak clearly from your heart • Communicate with courage and compassion • Heighten your awareness for deep listening • Enhance your ability to listen to people with different belief systems. 8 x 8, 160 pp, Illus., Quality PB, ISBN 1-893361-44-6 **$16.95**

Labyrinths from the Outside In
Walking to Spiritual Insight—a Beginner's Guide
by *Donna Schaper* and *Carole Ann Camp*

The user-friendly, interfaith guide to making and using labyrinths— for meditation, prayer, and celebration.

Labyrinth walking is a spiritual exercise *anyone* can do. This accessible guide unlocks the mysteries of the labyrinth for all of us, providing ideas for using the labyrinth walk for prayer, meditation, and celebrations to mark the most important moments in life. Includes instructions for making a labyrinth of your own and finding one in your area.
6 x 9, 208 pp, b/w illus. and photographs, Quality PB, ISBN 1-893361-18-7 **$16.95**

SkyLight Illuminations Series
Andrew Harvey, series editor

Offers today's spiritual seeker an enjoyable entry into the great classic texts of the world's spiritual traditions. Each classic is presented in an accessible translation, with facing pages of guided commentary from experts, giving you the keys you need to understand the history, context, and meaning of the text. This series enables readers of all backgrounds to experience and understand classic spiritual texts directly, and to make them a part of their lives. Andrew Harvey writes the foreword to each volume, an insightful, personal introduction to each classic.

Bhagavad Gita: *Annotated & Explained*
Translation by *Shri Purohit Swami*; Annotation by *Kendra Crossen Burroughs*

"The very best Gita for first-time readers." —Ken Wilber

Millions of people turn daily to India's most beloved holy book, whose universal appeal has made it popular with non-Hindus and Hindus alike. This edition introduces you to the characters; explains references and philosophical terms; shares the interpretations of famous spiritual leaders and scholars; and more. 5½ x 8½, 192 pp, Quality PB, ISBN 1-893361-28-4 **$16.95**

  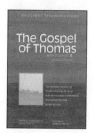

The Way of a Pilgrim: *Annotated & Explained*
Translation and annotation by *Gleb Pokrovsky*

The classic of Russian spirituality—now with facing-page commentary that illuminates and explains the text for you.

This delightful account is the story of one man who sets out to learn the prayer of the heart—also known as the "Jesus prayer"—and how the practice transforms his existence. This edition guides you through an abridged version of the text with facing-page annotations explaining the names, terms and references. 5½ x 8½, 160 pp, Quality PB, ISBN 1-893361-31-4 **$14.95**

The Gospel of Thomas: *Annotated & Explained*
Translation and annotation by *Stevan Davies*

The recently discovered mystical sayings of Jesus—now with facing-page commentary that illuminates and explains the text for you.

Discovered in 1945, this collection of aphoristic sayings sheds new light on the origins of Christianity and the intriguing figure of Jesus, portraying the Kingdom of God as a present fact about the world, rather than a future promise or future threat. This edition guides you through the text with annotations that focus on the meaning of the sayings, ideal for readers with no previous background in Christian history or thought.
5½ x 8½, 192 pp, Quality PB, ISBN 1-893361-45-4 **$15.95**

SkyLight Illuminations Series
Andrew Harvey, series editor

Zohar: *Annotated & Explained*
Translation and annotation by *Daniel C. Matt*

The cornerstone text of Kabbalah, now with facing-page commentary that illuminates and explains the text for you.

The best-selling author of *The Essential Kabbalah* brings together in one place the most important teachings of the *Zohar*, the canonical text of Jewish mystical tradition. Guides readers step by step through the midrash, mystical fantasy and Hebrew scripture that make up the *Zohar*, explaining the inner meanings in facing-page commentary. Ideal for readers without any prior knowledge of Jewish mysticism.

5½ x 8½, 176 pp, Quality PB, ISBN 1-893361-51-9 **$15.95**

 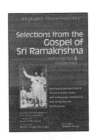 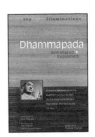

Selections from the Gospel of Sri Ramakrishna
Annotated & Explained
Translation by *Swami Nikhilananda*; Annotation by *Kendra Crossen Burroughs*

The words of India's greatest example of God-consciousness and mystical ecstasy in recent history—now with facing-page commentary that illuminates and explains the text for you.

Introduces the fascinating world of the Indian mystic and the universal appeal of his message that has inspired millions of devotees for more than a century. Selections from the original text and insightful yet unobtrusive commentary highlight the most important and inspirational teachings. Ideal for readers without any prior knowledge of Hinduism.

5½ x 8½, 240 pp, b/w photographs, Quality PB, ISBN 1-893361-46-2 **$16.95**

Dhammapada: *Annotated & Explained*
Translation by *Max Müller* and revised by *Jack Maguire*; Annotation by *Jack Maguire*

The classic of Buddhist spiritual practice—now with facing-page commentary that illuminates and explains the text for you.

The Dhammapada—words spoken by the Buddha himself over 2,500 years ago—is notoriously difficult to understand for the first-time reader. Now you can experience it with understanding even if you have no previous knowledge of Buddhism. Enlightening facing-page commentary explains all the names, terms, and references, giving you deeper insight into the text. An excellent introduction to Buddhist life and practice.

5½ x 8½, 160 pp, Quality PB, ISBN 1-893361-42-X **$14.95**

Meditation/Prayer

Finding Grace at the Center: *The Beginning of Centering Prayer*
by *M. Basil Pennington*, OCSO, *Thomas Keating*, OCSO, and *Thomas E. Clarke*, SJ

The book that helped launch the Centering Prayer "movement." Explains the prayer of *The Cloud of Unknowing*, posture and relaxation, the three simple rules of centering prayer, and how to cultivate centering prayer throughout all aspects of your life.
5 x 7¼,112 pp, HC, ISBN 1-893361-69-1 **$14.95**

Three Gates to Meditation Practice
A Personal Journey into Sufism, Buddhism, and Judaism
by *David A. Cooper*

Shows us how practicing within more than one spiritual tradition can lead us to our true home.

Here are over fifteen years from the journey of "post-denominational rabbi" David A. Cooper, author of *God Is a Verb*, and his wife, Shoshana—years in which the Coopers explored a rich variety of practices, from chanting Sufi *dhikr* to Buddhist Vipassanā meditation, to the study of Kabbalah and esoteric Judaism. Their experience demonstrates that the spiritual path is really completely within our reach, whoever we are, whatever we do—as long as we are willing to practice it. 5½ x 8½, 240 pp, Quality PB, ISBN 1-893361-22-5 **$16.95**

 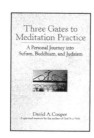  

Silence, Simplicity & Solitude
A Complete Guide to Spiritual Retreat at Home
by *David A. Cooper*

The classic personal spiritual retreat guide that enables readers to create their own self-guided spiritual retreat at home.

Award-winning author David Cooper traces personal mystical retreat in all of the world's major traditions, describing the varieties of spiritual practices for modern spiritual seekers. Cooper shares the techniques and practices that encompass the personal spiritual retreat experience, allowing readers to enhance their meditation practices and create an effective, self-guided spiritual retreat in their own homes—without the instruction of a meditation teacher. 5½ x 8½, 336 pp, Quality PB, ISBN 1-893361-04-7 **$16.95**

Prayer for People Who Think Too Much
A Guide to Everyday, Anywhere Prayer from the World's Faith Traditions
by *Mitch Finley*

Helps us make prayer a natural part of daily living.

Takes a thoughtful look at how each major faith tradition incorporates prayer into *daily* life. Explores Christian sacraments, Jewish holy days, Muslim daily prayer, "mindfulness" in Buddhism, and more, to help you better understand and enhance your own prayer practices. "I love this book." —Caroline M. Myss, Ph.D., author of *Anatomy of the Spirit*
5½ x 8½, 224 pp, Quality PB, ISBN 1-893361-21-7 **$16.95**; HC, ISBN 1-893361-00-4 **$21.95**

Children's Spirituality

Because Nothing Looks Like God

by *Lawrence and Karen Kushner*
Full-color illus. by
Dawn W. Majewski

For ages 4 & up

MULTICULTURAL, NONDENOMINATIONAL, NONSECTARIAN

Real-life examples of happiness and sadness—from goodnight stories, to the hope and fear felt the first time at bat, to the closing moments of life—introduce children to the possibilities of spiritual life. A vibrant way for children—and their adults—to explore what, where, and how God is in our lives.

11 x 8½, 32 pp, HC, Full-color illus., ISBN 1-58023-092-X **$16.95**

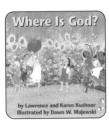

Where Is God? (A Board Book)

For ages 0–4

by *Lawrence and Karen Kushner*; Full-color illus. by *Dawn W. Majewski*

A gentle way for young children to explore how God is with us every day, in every way. Abridged from *Because Nothing Looks Like God* by Lawrence and Karen Kushner and specially adapted to board book format to delight and inspire young readers.

5 x 5, 24 pp, Board, Full-color illus., ISBN 1-893361-17-9 **$7.95**

What Does God Look Like? (A Board Book)

For ages 0–4

by *Lawrence and Karen Kushner*; Full-color illus. by *Dawn W. Majewski*

A simple way for young children to explore the ways that we "see" God. Abridged from *Because Nothing Looks Like God* by Lawrence and Karen Kushner and specially adapted to board book format to delight and inspire young readers.

5 x 5, 24 pp, Board, Full-color illus., ISBN 1-893361-23-3 **$7.95**

How Does God Make Things Happen? (A Board Book)

For ages 0–4

by *Lawrence and Karen Kushner*; Full-color illus. by *Dawn W. Majewski*

A charming invitation for young children to explore how God makes things happen in our world. Abridged from *Because Nothing Looks Like God* by Lawrence and Karen Kushner and specially adapted to board book format to delight and inspire young readers.

5 x 5, 24 pp, Board, Full-color illus., ISBN 1-893361-24-1 **$7.95**

What Is God's Name? (A Board Book)

For ages 0–4

by *Sandy Eisenberg Sasso*; Full-color illus. by *Phoebe Stone*

Everyone and everything in the world has a name. What is God's name? Abridged from the award-winning *In God's Name* by Sandy Eisenberg Sasso and specially adapted to board book format to delight and inspire young readers.

5 x 5, 24 pp, Board, Full-color illus., ISBN 1-893361-10-1 **$7.95**

Children's Spirituality

Where Does God Live?

For ages 3–6

by *August Gold* and *Matthew J. Perlman*

Using simple, everyday examples that children can relate to, this colorful book helps young readers develop a personal understanding of God.

10 x 8½, 32 pp, Quality PB, Full-color photo illus., ISBN 1-893361-39-X **$7.95**

God in Between

For ages 4 & up

by *Sandy Eisenberg Sasso*; Full-color illus. by *Sally Sweetland*

If you wanted to find God, where would you look? A magical, mythical tale that teaches that God can be found where we are: within all of us and the relationships between us. "This happy and wondrous book takes our children on a sweet and holy journey into God's presence." —Rabbi Wayne Dosick, Ph.D., author of *The Business Bible* and *Soul Judaism*

9 x 12, 32 pp, HC, Full-color illus., ISBN 1-879045-86-9 **$16.95**

Cain & Abel: *Finding the Fruits of Peace*

For ages 5 & up

by *Sandy Eisenberg Sasso*; Full-color illus. by *Joani Keller Rothenberg*

A sensitive recasting of the ancient tale shows we have the power to deal with anger in positive ways. Provides questions for kids and adults to explore together. "Editor's Choice"—American Library Association's *Booklist* 9 x 12, 32 pp, HC, Full-color illus., ISBN 1-58023-123-3 **$16.95**

In Our Image: *God's First Creatures*

For ages 4 & up

by *Nancy Sohn Swartz*; Full-color illus. by *Melanie Hall*

A playful new twist on the Creation story—from the perspective of the animals. Celebrates the interconnectedness of nature and the harmony of all living things. "The vibrantly colored illustrations nearly leap off the page in this delightful interpretation." —*School Library Journal*
"A message all children should hear, presented in words and pictures that children will find irresistible." —Rabbi Harold Kushner, author of *When Bad Things Happen to Good People*

9 x 12, 32 pp, HC, Full-color illus., ISBN 1-879045-99-0 **$16.95**

Children's Spirituality

Ten Amazing People
And How They Changed the World
by *Maura D. Shaw*; Foreword by *Dr. Robert Coles*
Full-color illus. by *Stephen Marchesi*

For ages 6–10

Black Elk • Dorothy Day • Malcolm X • Mahatma Gandhi • Martin Luther King, Jr. • Mother Teresa • Janusz Korczak • Desmond Tutu • Thich Nhat Hanh • Albert Schweitzer

This vivid, inspirational, and authoritative book will open new possibilities for children by telling the stories of how ten of the past century's greatest leaders changed the world in important ways.
8½, x 11, 48 pp, HC, Full-color illus., ISBN 1-893361-47-0 **$17.95**

God's Paintbrush
by *Sandy Eisenberg Sasso*; Full-color illus. by *Annette Compton*

For ages 4 & up

Invites children of all faiths and backgrounds to encounter God openly in their own lives. Wonderfully interactive; provides questions adult and child can explore together at the end of each episode. "An excellent way to honor the imaginative breadth and depth of the spiritual life of the young." —Dr. Robert Coles, Harvard University
11 x 8½, 32 pp, HC, Full-color illus., ISBN 1-879045-22-2 **$16.95**

Also available:
A Teacher's Guide 8½ x 11, 32 pp, PB, ISBN 1-879045-57-5 **$8.95**
God's Paintbrush Celebration Kit 9½ x 12, HC, Includes 5 sessions/40 full-color Activity Sheets and Teacher Folder with complete instructions, ISBN 1-58023-050-4 **$21.95**

In God's Name
by *Sandy Eisenberg Sasso*; Full-color illus. by *Phoebe Stone*

For ages 4 & up

Like an ancient myth in its poetic text and vibrant illustrations, this award-winning modern fable about the search for God's name celebrates the diversity and, at the same time, the unity of all the people of the world. "What a lovely, healing book!" —Madeleine L'Engle
9 x 12, 32 pp, HC, Full-color illus., ISBN 1-879045-26-5 **$16.95**

Also available in Spanish:
El nombre de Dios 9 x 12, 32 pp, HC, Full-color illus., ISBN 1-893361-63-2 **$16.95**

God Said Amen
by *Sandy Eisenberg Sasso*; Full-color illus. by *Avi Katz*

For ages 4 & up

Inspiring tale of two kingdoms: one overflowing with water but without oil to light its lamps; the other blessed with oil but no water to grow its gardens. The kingdoms' rulers ask God for help but are too stubborn to ask each other. Shows that we need only reach out to each other to find God's answer to our prayers. 9 x 12, 32 pp, HC, Full-color illus., ISBN 1-58023-080-6 **$16.95**

Spirituality

Journeys of Simplicity
Traveling Light with Thomas Merton, Bashō, Edward Abbey, Annie Dillard & Others
by *Philip Harnden*

There is a more graceful way of traveling through life.

Offers vignettes of forty "travelers" and the few ordinary things they carried with them—from place to place, from day to day, from birth to death. What Thoreau took to Walden Pond. What Thomas Merton packed for his final trip to Asia. What Annie Dillard keeps in her writing tent. What an impoverished cook served M. F. K. Fisher for dinner. Much more.

"'How much should I carry with me?' is the quintessential question for any journey, especially the journey of life. Herein you'll find sage, sly, wonderfully subversive advice."
—Bill McKibben, author of *The End of Nature*

5 x 7¼, 128 pp, HC, ISBN 1-893361-76-4 **$16.95**

The Alphabet of Paradise
An A–Z of Spirituality for Everyday Life
by *Howard Cooper*

"An extraordinary book." —Karen Armstrong

One of the most eloquent new voices in spirituality, Howard Cooper takes us on a journey of discovery—into ourselves and into the past—to find the signposts that can help us live more meaningful lives. In twenty-six engaging chapters—from A to Z—Cooper spiritually illuminates the subjects of daily life, using an ancient Jewish mystical method of interpretation that reveals both the literal and more allusive meanings of each. Topics include: Awe, Bodies, Creativity, Dreams, Emotions, Sports, and more.

5 x 7¾, 224 pp, Quality PB, ISBN 1-893361-80-2 **$16.95**

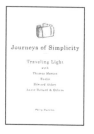
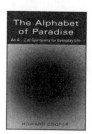

Winter
A Spiritual Biography of the Season
Edited by *Gary Schmidt* and *Susan M. Felch;* Illustrations by *Barry Moser*

Explore how the dormancy of winter can be a time of spiritual preparation and transformation.

In thirty stirring pieces, *Winter* delves into the varied feelings that winter conjures in us, calling up both the barrenness and the beauty of the natural world in wintertime. Includes selections by Will Campbell, Rachel Carson, Annie Dillard, Donald Hall, Ron Hansen, Jane Kenyon, Jamaica Kincaid, Barry Lopez, Kathleen Norris, John Updike, E. B. White, and many others.

"This outstanding anthology features top-flight nature and spirituality writers on the fierce, inexorable season of winter.... Remarkably lively and warm, despite the icy subject."
—★*Publishers Weekly* Starred Review

6 x 9, 288 pp, 6 b/w illus., HC, ISBN 1-893361-53-5 **$21.95**